More Than Letters

Literacy Activities for Preschool, Kindergarten, and First Grade

by
Sally Moomaw
and
Brenda Hieronymus

Redleaf Press

Published by: Redleaf Press
            a division of Resources for Child Caring
            450 N. Syndicate, Suite 5
            St. Paul, MN 55104

Distributed by: Gryphon House
            Mailing Address:
            P.O. Box 207
            Beltsville, MD 20704-0207

ISBN 1-884834-98-1

Library of Congress Cataloging-in-Publication Data
Moomaw, Sally, 1948-
     More than letters : literacy activities for preschool, kindergarten,
 and first grade / by Sally Moomaw and Brenda Hieronymus.
        p. cm.
     Includes bibliographical references.
     ISBN 1-884834-98-1
      1. Language arts (Early childhood) 2. Language experience
 approach in education. 3. Early childhood education—Activity
 programs. I. Hieronymus, Brenda, 1945- . II. Title.
 LB1139.5.L35 M66 2001
 372.6—dc21
                                            00-068428

To Mary Ann McPherson, Sharon Harris Griffin,
and Diane Blackburn, who were so instrumental
in helping us understand emergent literacy and
so helpful with their ideas for materials.

Acknowledgments

We thank the Arlitt Child and Family Research and Education Center at the University of Cincinnati for its continued support. Many of the photographs in this book feature the facilities, equipment, materials, and children from the center. In particular, we thank the Arlitt teachers, both past and current, for sharing their wonderful ideas and insights.

We again thank David C. Baxter for his extensive time spent photographing children and materials for this book. David has been with us for all six of the *More Than . . .* books, and we greatly appreciate his contribution.

Special thanks go to Charles Moomaw for his computer and technical support throughout the preparation of this manuscript, as well as the previous five books. His patience and emotional support are also greatly appreciated.

We express our heartfelt appreciation to the staff at Redleaf Press for working so hard to make the *More Than . . .* series a reality and for giving us a forum to share our curriculum ideas with others in the early childhood field. In particular, we thank our editor, Beth Wallace, who has worked with us on our last three books.

Finally, we thank the children who helped us with the photos for this book: Elias, Natasha, Will, Andrew, Bonnie, Eden, Elina, Heqing, Joshua, Justis, Karen, Kevin, Lexis, Lonnasia, Nikhil, Richard, Safira, Shannon, Sijia, Yao, Zach, Casey, Alexander, and Zoya.

Contents

Preface

More Than Letters is an extensive compilation of emergent-literacy materials and activities that translate theory and research into a dynamic, effective literacy program for children from preschool through first grade. The curriculum has evolved over the past two decades following the emergence of the whole-language movement and renewed interest in how young children construct literacy concepts. In collaboration with interested faculty and teachers at the University of Cincinnati's Arlitt Child and Family Research and Education Center, teachers began to design and incorporate a variety of literacy materials into their preschool and kindergarten classrooms. They carefully observed how children interacted with the materials, recorded growth and learning, and discarded or modified unsuccessful materials. The results were startling. Where previously few of the preschool children had engaged in reading and writing activities other than listening to books, teachers soon noticed an active interest in print, as well as emergent reading and writing skills, in virtually all of the children.

Of course, not all of the attempts at designing literacy materials were successful. Initially, there were as many failures as successes. It quickly became apparent that some types of activities encouraged children to interact with print, while others were largely ignored. For example, children showed little interest in labels on equipment in the classroom or in matching key words to charts. On the other hand, they were very interested in charts derived from popular songs or predictable books that allowed them to add or change important words. *More Than Letters* contains more than 100 of the most successful materials and activities.

For quite some time there has been a heated debate among educators regarding the most effective way to teach reading and writing. Should teachers use a whole-language approach or incorporate more direct instruction about phonics? In our classrooms, we have consistently observed that children construct phonetic concepts out of their extensive explorations of print. Certainly teachers have an important role to play. On the one hand, by facilitating phonetic awareness as children explore print-rich materials, teachers help them construct the relationship between particular letters or groups of letters and the sounds they produce. Similarly, as teachers encourage children to play with the sounds of the language, perhaps through rhymes or games, they help children develop phonemic awareness, or the ability to distinguish the individual sounds (phonemes) that make up a word. On the other hand, isolating phonetics (the relationship between the letters or patterns of letters and the sounds they represent) from real language experiences does not seem effective in helping children develop the relationship between oral and written language. For this reason, *More Than Letters* features an extensive whole-language curriculum that readers can use to create classroom environments that surround children with meaningful print. In addition, with each activity we have provided specific suggestions for comments and questions that teachers can use to encourage phonetic awareness.

Terminology is important for early childhood teachers to understand, but it can also become cumbersome. In the area of reading, the terms *phonemic* and *phonetic* are frequently used. For ease of reading, in this book we have typically grouped both *phonemic* and *phonetic* under the more global term, *phonetic*. Since teachers often draw children's attention to the letters or groups of letters that represent the sounds children isolate, *phonetic* seems the more appropriate choice.

When discussing reading, educators often talk about *sound–symbol* or *sound–letter relationships*. In his book *Phonics Phacts,* author and educator Ken Goodman argues that such designations are inaccurate since sounds are also symbols (Portsmouth, NH: Heinemann, 1993). While we agree with his argument, we have chosen to use these familiar designations because they are so commonly used in the professional literature. However, we certainly agree that sounds are also symbols and that strict sound-to-letter relationships are often simplifications of more complex phonetic relationships.

Jean Piaget described spoken language as a system of arbitrary signs. He used the term *sign* to designate representations, such as letters or words, that bear no resemblance to what they represent. He used the term *symbol* to refer to representations that do look like what they represent, such as the image of a person walking that we see at pedestrian crossings. In this book, we have used the more general term *symbol* when referring to letters and words because this term is more familiar to many readers.

Literacy does not develop in isolation from other areas of learning. Opportunities for literacy development extend to all areas of the classroom. For this reason, we have not limited our activities to the book or writing centers of the classroom. Ideas for encouraging emergent reading and writing in the dramatic play, art, music, manipulative, block, science, and sensory table areas are included. In addition, each activity includes suggestions for integrated curriculum activities. Since many teachers have informed us that they like to coordinate activities from the books in this curriculum series, many of the integrated curriculum sections refer readers to specific activities from the other *More Than* books published by Redleaf Press: *More Than Counting* (1995), *More Than Magnets* (1997), *More Than Singing* (1997), *More Than Painting* (1999), and *Much More Than Counting* (1999). There are also suggestions for modifying each activity to make it more complex or less difficult. In this way, teachers can design activities to meet the needs of individual children or of their group.

More Than Letters follows the format of the other books in the *More Than . . .* series. Each chapter highlights questions teachers often pose related to particular literacy activities. Each activity includes a photograph that shows the materials and how to present them attractively. Included with each activity are clear directions for making or assembling the materials, guidelines for the most appropriate age levels, a list of specific materials, suggestions for what to expect as children use the materials, comments and questions to extend thinking and phonetic awareness, and modifications to enhance the activity or to change the level of difficulty.

Throughout the book, we refer to *teachers* and their role in facilitating children's literacy development. The term *teacher* is meant to be inclusive. All those who work with young children are teachers, whether they are parents, child care workers, or classroom aides. This book is designed to meet the needs of a wide spectrum of people who care for and nurture young children.

The activities in this book are designed for preschool, kindergarten, and first-grade children, age three and older. Some of the materials contain small pieces. A teacher whose children still put things in their mouths should use pieces that young children cannot swallow.

All of the activities that appear in *More Than Letters* have been field-tested in classrooms at the Arlitt Child and Family Research and Education Center at the University of Cincinnati in Ohio. The children enrolled in the center come from diverse family backgrounds. Some are funded by Head Start, some pay tuition, and others are funded through an agency for children with disabilities. Many are learning English as a second language. All of the children are able to use these materials to extend their literacy growth.

Literacy is one of the most important areas of education. Early enjoyment of reading and writing provides a foundation for a lifetime of ongoing learning. It is our hope that the ideas in this book will help teachers guide children as they discover the wonders of reading and writing.

The Literacy-Rich Classroom

When does reading and writing start? Are preschool children too young to engage in reading and writing activities? Take a peek into a classroom of three- to five-year-old children and see:

- *Several children sit with their teacher at the special activity table. She writes what they tell her about the pictures they have drawn. The pages will be compiled into a class book.*

- *In the reading area, three children cluster around a popular book with a repeating text and recite the words together.*

- *Nearby, a child points to the words on a class chart and chooses a card with his best friend's name to add to the chart.*

- *A little girl arrives with her father. She runs to the teacher and shows her the writing she did with the take-home literacy suitcase.*

- *In the manipulative area, a child arranges magnetic letters to spell* Mom *and* Dad.

- *In the dramatic play area, two children write down grocery orders as they pretend to talk on the phone.*

- *In the block area, a child uses invented spelling to write a* Save *sign for her block structure.*

- *In the writing center, one child copies word cards into a blank book while another types words on a computer.*

▲ ▲ ▲

In literacy-rich classrooms, children are surrounded by opportunities to interact with print in ways that are meaningful to them. The transition into reading and writing occurs naturally as they experiment with written language. Years of experience in our diverse classrooms have shown that this occurs for all children, regardless of cultural or socioeconomic backgrounds. In fact, children learning English as a second language have progressed into written language concurrently with learning to speak English.

Literacy and the Young Child

As children are exposed to written language, both through books and through print in their environment, they begin to construct important literacy concepts.[1] For example, they learn that what is spoken can also be written, and that there is a prescribed way for writing things down. Children who do not yet understand the relationship between spoken and written language may appear puzzled if the teacher says she will write down what they say. However, repeated opportunities to see spoken words in written form help children construct the relationship between oral and written language. They learn that once something is written, it says the same thing no matter who reads it.

As children continue to explore books, they learn to distinguish the pictures from the print. They also observe the left-to-right and top-to-bottom progression of the text, notice the configuration of words, and begin to recognize the function of letters in the formation of words. Children develop both *phonemic* and *phonetic* awareness. *Phonemic awareness* refers to the ability to recognize spoken words as a sequence of sounds, while *phonetic awareness* describes an understanding of the relationship between letters (or groups of letters) and the sounds they represent. Eventually, children begin to recognize certain words and make the transition into actual reading. The process of reading evolves from the whole to the part.[2] In other words, children first differentiate the print from the rest of the page globally. Later, they begin to distinguish words from the stream of writing, and finally they look at the parts of the words as they form letter–sound relationships.

Children also follow a predictable progression in learning to write, much as they move through stages in learning to speak.[3] When surrounded by meaningful writing, children naturally transition into writing themselves, just as they progress in speaking through living in a verbal environment. While the rate of development in writing varies from child to child, the sequence of the stages follows a predictable order. This seems to be the case regardless of the child's native language. In our classrooms, we have observed similar stages emerge in children transitioning into writing in Chinese, Arabic, and English.

Writing Stages
Stage 1—Scribbling

Scribbling represents a child's first attempt at reproducing writing. While similar to the scribbling stage in art, the marks children create to represent writing are often more controlled. Scribbling is similar to babbling in oral language. While babbling allows children to explore the sounds of language, scribbling enables them to experiment with the visual appearance of writing.

Stage 1 Examples: Scribbling

Stage 2—Linear/Repetitive Drawing

This stage is sometimes referred to as *personal cursive*. At this level, children's scribbling has been refined to look much more like standard writing. In fact, teachers who are not familiar with a child's native language may mistake the child's personal cursive for actual writing (see the Stage 2 example from a child of a Chinese family). As with scribbling, this stage of development in writing parallels early refinements in speaking. As children progress in learning to speak, they gradually drop sounds that are not present in their own language and retain only the relevant sounds. In a similar manner, as children become more aware of how writing actually looks, they refine their own writing attempts.

Stage 2 Examples: Personal Cursive

from an English-speaking child   *from a Chinese-speaking child*

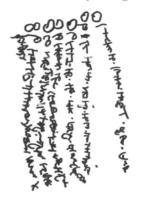

Stage 3—Letterlike Forms

At this stage, children's writing looks very close to actual printing; in fact, many of the marks may look almost like letters. As children progress to the next stage of writing, teachers may observe letters and letterlike forms intermingled in their writing.

Stage 3 Example: Letterlike Forms

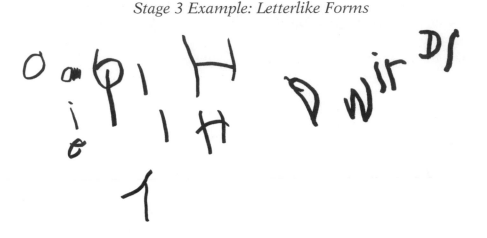

Stage 4—Letters and Early Word-Symbol Relationships

Children at this stage are beginning to reproduce letters and often use a single letter to represent an entire word. While the letters may not all be formed correctly, there may be a one-to-one correspondence between the number of letters written and the number of words they represent. This is similar to an early stage of speaking when children use a single word to represent an entire thought, such as "Out" for "I want to go outside." At this stage, the child indicates a clearer intent for the letters to represent specific words than in Stage 3.

Stage 4 Example: Word-Symbols

Don't take robot
—Quentin

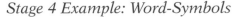

Stage 5—Invented Spelling

As children move into this stage of writing, they clearly demonstrate that they have constructed some sound–letter relationships. The first sounds that children usually represent are initial consonants. Later, more consonants are added, and finally vowels. While they may leave out some sounds or may represent some sounds with the incorrect letter, children at this level show a substantial amount of knowledge about the structure of words. Phonics errors are similar to the overgeneralizations that children often make when speaking, such as saying "mouses" for "mice" after learning the general rule of adding an "s" to form plurals. Such mistakes actually show that they have constructed significant knowledge about grammatical rules. In the first Stage 5 example, the child initially writes his message using mostly consonants. Several weeks later, he writes the same message but adds more vowels, though not always the correct ones.

Stage 5 Examples: Invented Spelling

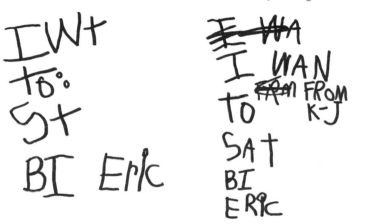

*I want to
sit by Eric.*

*Dear Sally,
How was your March?
I liked my March.
Love,
Lee Ann*

Stage 6—Standard Spelling

Eventually, children realize that words have a standard spelling. Even in preschool, some children remember the spellings of certain familiar words, such as *mom, dad, cat, love,* or their names.

Stage 6 Examples: Standard Spelling

I LIKe ice cream And The Butter FLy is Back

I Want to Sit Next to DanielW

Children may revert to earlier stages of writing when they have a lot to say. After all, personal cursive is much faster than actually writing letters or words. Thus, the teacher may observe long strands of personal cursive or letterlike forms punctuated by significant words.

Example of personal cursive alongside names of family members

Mom, Dad, Caroline

Classroom environments that provide materials and relevant models encourage children to progress through the writing stages.

Literacy and the Early Childhood Teacher

Teachers of young children encourage the emergence of reading and writing by creating classroom environments that surround children with meaningful print. This is often referred to as a *whole-language* approach. Context is important. When letters or phonics are isolated from meaningful words or phrases, children cannot form the important relationship between oral and written language. While they may memorize rules or sounds, the experience lacks real meaning. However, when word boundaries, letters, and sounds are explored within a context that has meaning, such as a repeating phrase from a popular song or book, children relate the words and letters they see to the sounds they hear. The following anecdote illustrates the problem of trying to teach phonics outside of a meaningful print context.

A five-year-old child entered school during the middle of the year. At his previous school, he had been instructed about the sounds of various letters. His new class was compiling a book of stories to accompany pictures they had drawn. When it was the new child's turn, he asked the teacher how she would know what to write on his page. "I'll write down what you tell me," she replied. The child was confused and repeated his question several times. Finally, the teacher explained, "There's a way to write down all the words you say. I know how to do that, and I'll show you how it looks." While the child had memorized sounds to accompany letters, the knowledge had no practical meaning to him because he had not yet had the opportunity to construct the relationship between written and oral language.

Facilitating Emergent Reading

Teachers can help children understand and decode written language by

- carefully selecting books to share with them
- providing many opportunities for children to interact with print
- extending stories and written language into other areas of the curriculum

Through book sharing, children begin to understand book language and the important components of a story. When teachers select a variety of types of books, children's learning opportunities are extended. For example, *predictable books,* which have a repeating text or some other element that establishes a predictable pattern, allow children to quickly memorize the words and anticipate what will come next. Children can tell the story along with the teacher and begin to feel like readers. Nonpredictable books, on the other hand, provide a more extensive use of language and description, which increases children's vocabulary and language development. Books with rhyme and rhythm encourage children to play with language and to focus on similarities and differences in the sounds of words. Informational books may pique children's curiosity and increase their knowledge of the world, while multicultural books allow them to consider the similarities, as well as the differences, among peoples.

Children focus more carefully on written language when they have many opportunities to manipulate print. Movable alphabets, word games, and charts with movable words are some of the many curriculum activities teachers can design to increase children's interactions with print.

Through play, children create a network of relationships and extend their understanding of the world. By introducing book topics into other areas of the curriculum, teachers allow children to use their play skills to interpret stories more fully. For example, many children enjoy the silly book *The Lady with the Alligator Purse.*[4] By incorporating a few props from the book into the dramatic play area, such as toy pizzas and doctors' bags, teachers encourage children to reenact the story, perhaps with their own variations. Similarly, many children are attracted to Jan Brett's book *The Mitten.*[5] They love to recreate the story with small plastic animals and a mitten. In the process, they practice following the sequence of a story and have many opportunities to consolidate new vocabulary, such as the names of the various animals.

Children's exposure to reading is certainly not limited to books. Children see writing in many contexts throughout their day, from signs to cereal boxes to junk mail. Teachers can increase children's exposure to meaningful print by incorporating examples throughout the classroom. Food containers and phone books in the dramatic play area, road signs in the block area, and interactive song charts in the music area are just a few examples.

Facilitating Emergent Writing

Teachers also play an important role in encouraging the emergence of writing in young children. Strategies to facilitate the development of writing include

- accepting all writing as valid
- breaking down words and letters into more manageable parts
- providing appropriate models and many opportunities to write

Once teachers understand the sequence of development of children's writing, they can accept all writing attempts as part of a developmental process. By validating children's early attempts at writing, teachers encourage them to continue the process. Right from the beginning, children can feel competent as writers.

Some children progress more quickly in developing writing skills when teachers scaffold by isolating parts of letters or words for them. While young children may be eager to copy certain words, such as their names, the task may seem too confusing and formidable for some. Teachers can help by focusing on individual letters within the context of a word and by giving verbal clues for how to make them. Teachers must judge carefully when to assist children in writing. Children need many opportunities to manipulate writing tools before they are ready for refinements.

Children are encouraged to write when there is a reason for it. When teachers supply appropriate models, such as word cards from a favorite story or topic, children are naturally motivated to reproduce them. By supplying writing materials in all areas of the classroom, teachers encourage children to incorporate writing as a regular part of their play. Writing restaurant orders, recording scores from a target game, writing observations for what may be inside a coconut, or creating labels for block structures are some of the many ways that children may incorporate writing throughout the classroom.

Literacy and the Early Childhood Classroom

Literacy-rich classrooms encourage children to explore written language throughout the day and in many areas of the classroom. The opportunities are endless, and many possibilities are described in the activity chapters of this book. The following lists summarize the types of activities that promote reading and writing throughout the classroom.

Reading across the Curriculum

- *Attendance charts* help children learn to recognize the printed forms of their names and their classmates' names as they look for the appropriate name tags to hang on the chart. Activities 7.2 and 7.3 are examples.

- *Big books* are enlarged-print versions of predictable books, poems, or songs. They encourage children to focus on the relationship between spoken and written language. Chapter 2 discusses big books in detail.

- *Interactive charts* allow children to manipulate certain key words within the context of a predictable text. Chapter 3 gives many examples of interactive charts.

- *Name tags* build on children's natural interest in how their own names look, as well as the names of their classmates. Activity 7.1 shows a variety of ways for using name tags.

- *Message boards* help reinforce the concept that print conveys meaning. Activities 7.16 and 7.17 describe different types of message boards.

- *Word banks* give children the opportunity to see the words that are most interesting to them in print. Word banks and their variations are described in activities 6.1 through 6.4.

- *Project documentation,* which allows children to see their thoughts and words in writing, is a useful tool for helping them remember past experiences and organize further explorations. In Activity 4.11, children document a field trip to a pumpkin patch with photographs and words.

- *Environmental print*—signs, labels, and other printed material—permeates literacy-rich classrooms. Chapter 7 explores many uses of environmental print throughout the classroom.

- *Dictation,* in which teachers write down children's stories or ideas exactly as they are expressed, is a useful tool for helping children understand the relationship between spoken and written language. Activity 4.3 discusses dictation.

- *Manipulative games* encourage children to move letters or words into various configurations to convey meaning. Chapter 6 includes many examples of manipulative games.

- *Group games* allow children to share information within a game context. Activities 6.3, 6.5, 6.7, and 6.8 are examples of group literacy games.

- *Transition songs* enable teachers to focus on children's names, initial letters in names, and sound–letter relationships within a meaningful context. Activity 3.1 is an example.

Writing Across the Curriculum

- *Writing centers* are specific areas within classrooms that encourage writing by providing interesting writing materials and appropriate models. Chapter 5 describes many different writing centers.

- *Class books* allow each child to contribute an individual page to a group book. Sometimes the basic text is predictable but allows children to make small changes. Activity 4.12 is an example of a group book.

- *Pocket stories* encourage children to explore word boundaries and the relationship between spoken and written language. Children dictate a sentence to go with a picture they create. Duplicate words can be matched to the words in their sentence and stored in the pocket at the bottom of the page. Activity 4.1 describes pocket stories.

- *Writing caddies* containing basic writing materials, such as paper, pencil, and markers, can be placed around the classroom to encourage writing across the curriculum. Activity 4.18 discusses various writing boxes.

- *Sentence fill-ins* allow children to experiment with writing by adding a word or phrase to a predictable text. Children can observe how their writing alters the meaning of the original text. Many of the writing centers in chapter 5 feature sentence fill-ins.

- *Journal writing* is common in many kindergartens. Journals allow teachers and children to trace writing progress over an extended period. Activity 4.15 discusses journal writing.

- *Writing on interactive charts* enables children to experiment with the way writing conveys meaning. Children can write a word or phrase to add to the interactive part of the chart. Activity 3.10 is an example.

- *Literacy suitcases* extend the literacy curriculum from school to home. Literacy suitcases are take-home versions of classroom writing materials. Chapter 8 describes a variety of literacy suitcases that teachers can create.

Goals for Reading and Writing

Goals for early childhood literacy programs emerge from an understanding of how children construct reading and writing concepts. The needs of individual children, including their strengths, interests, and learning styles, affect how general program goals are designed and implemented. Literacy goals for early childhood programs should include the following:

- developing children's familiarity with and enjoyment of books and reading
- providing many opportunities for children to interact with print
- fostering the construction of letter–sound relationships and letter–word relationships within a meaningful context
- enhancing vocabulary development
- supporting children's construction of literacy concepts, such as the relationship between spoken and written words
- nurturing children's emergent reading and writing skills
- facilitating reading and writing across the curriculum
- expanding children's understanding of book language
- encouraging children's feelings of competency in reading and writing

These goals encourage the active involvement of children in the reading and writing process. Teachers can design materials and activities to coordinate with other aspects of the classroom curriculum. In this way, the literacy curriculum both supports and is supported by the overall classroom curriculum.

1. Susan B. Neuman, Carol Copple, and Sue Bredekamp, *Learning to Read and Write* (Washington, DC: NAEYC, 2000) 14.
2. Ken Goodman, *What's Whole in Whole Language?* (Portsmouth, NH: Heineman, 1986) 9.
3. The description of writing development in this section is discussed in more detail in Marjorie V. Fields, "Talking and Writing: Explaining the Whole Language Approach to Parents," *The Reading Teacher,* May 1988: 898-903.
4. Nadine Bernard Westcott, *The Lady with the Alligator Purse* (Boston: Little Brown, 1988).
5. Jan Brett, *The Mitten* (New York: Putnam, 1989).

CHAPTER 2

With a bow-wow here,
Bow-wow there,
Here a bow,
There a wow,
Everywhere a bow-wow

Big Books

Momoko carefully looked at the words in the big-book version of Brown Bear, Brown Bear, What Do You See? *Although she had only recently come to the United States and did not yet speak much English, she remembered some of the animal names from the book. Each time the teacher read the book at group time, the children chanted along. Suddenly Momoko darted across the room to the writing center and brought back word cards that had pictures and names of the animal characters from the book. She carefully began to place the word card for each animal under the corresponding word in the big book.*

▲ ▲ ▲

Dimitri listened as the teacher read the big book I Went Walking *during group time. It was one of his favorite stories. Later in the day, he took the regular-size version of the book from the book- shelf and found the same book in board-book format at the writing center. Dimitri asked the teacher if he could also look at the big book. Sitting on the floor, Dimitri opened each of the three versions of the book to the same page and carefully began comparing them.*

▲ ▲ ▲

Listening to familiar books introduces children to important components of written language. As they listen to the same words each time a story is read, children naturally begin to make com- parisons between the words they hear and how those words look in the book. Big books allow teachers to share the intimacy of small-group book sharing with a larger group of children.

Teachers' Questions

What are "big books"?

Big books are enlarged-print versions of predictable books, poems, or songs. The words are printed in large letters so that children can easily see them as the teacher reads. Being able to compare the written and spoken language helps children form important literacy relationships.

Why are big books an important component of the early childhood literacy curriculum?

Big books facilitate children's construction of important concepts about written language, such as

- *sound–symbol relationships*
- *voice–print pairing*
- *boundaries of words*
- *left-to-right and top-to-bottom text progression*
- *use of upper- and lowercase letters*

As children transition into reading, they must construct the **sound–symbol relationship** between the sounds, or *phonemes,* in a word and the way they are represented in print. They must also learn to pair each spoken word with a written counterpart *(voice–print pairing).* When teachers carefully point to each word in a big book as they read it, children begin to form these important relationships. They also begin to discern the **boundaries of words** and the significance of the space between two words. With repeated readings of big books and the chance to see the teacher pointing to the text as she reads, children gradually realize that the text is always read from **left to right** and from **top to bottom.** They learn to distinguish **upper- and lowercase letters** and may begin to recognize how uppercase letters are used. For example, many young children realize that names start with a capital letter.

What criteria should teachers consider when selecting big books?

Teachers should evaluate both the content and the appearance of the text when selecting big books. The text should be predictable, using words that repeat or are strongly suggested by the illustrations. This enables children to quickly remember the spoken words and compare them to their written counterparts. The print should be a standard style, such as is typically used in books for children. It should be uniform in size and large enough for all children to see clearly when they are seated at group time. There should be enough space between the words so that children can easily tell where one word stops and the next one starts.

Where can teachers get big books?

Teachers can buy or make big books. Commercial big books are available in early-childhood catalogs, bookstores, and

Internet Web sites. Teachers can make their own big books using large construction paper and sentence strips.

What are the drawbacks of some commercial big books?

The length and content of the text, as well as the size and style of print in many commercial big books, do not support the goals of early literacy programs. Many publishers adapt nonpredictable children's books to big-book format. While children may enjoy listening to the stories, they cannot remember or predict the text and thus cannot establish relationships between the written and spoken words. In addition, commercial big books often have print that is too small for children in large-group situations to see. Children cannot construct knowledge about printed language when they cannot clearly see it. Finally, commercial big books are often less durable than big books constructed by teachers.

How can teachers make their own big books?

The easiest way to make big books is to cut out the illustrations from two paperback copies of a book and print the words on sentence strips, lined strips of paper approximately 2 feet long. This allows the teacher to enlarge the print while retaining the original illustrations. (Since most books have illustrations on both the front and the back of each page, two copies are needed to recover all of the illustrations.) Both the pictures and the sentence strips can be adhered to twelve-by-eighteen-inch construction paper and laminated for durability. Teachers can also make big books by printing directly onto construction paper and drawing their own illustrations, or they can print the text in a large type size on a computer. It helps to set the page layout to "landscape," so that the lines print sideways and can be longer. Teachers should select a font that is as close as possible to standard print, such as Arial or Helvetica.

What are good source materials for big books?

Predictable books, songs, and poems that are of high interest to children are good sources of text for big books. In each case, children are likely to memorize the words quickly and "read" along with the teacher. Their interest in the text and familiarity with the words allow them to focus on the written version and draw conclusions. Since many children remember words even more easily when they are sung, songs often make excellent big books.

Which predictable books convert best into big books?

Books that have a repeating line of text, with one or two word changes per page, are good choices. Books with rhyming words also work well. Both types of book encourage children to look closely at the print and notice similarities and differences. When the same text repeats, children learn to distinguish changes in the text. When books include rhyme, children look for slight differences in words that sound almost alike. See appendix A for a list of suggested predictable books.

What should teachers consider when making big books?

Teachers should give primary consideration to enlarging the print and fitting the text onto the page. The size of the illustrations is less important than the size of the print. Since teachers will be pointing to the words as they read, putting the text at the top of the page when possible allows them to point to the words without covering up the illustrations. Teachers should be careful to include a relatively large space between words. The pages can be laminated for durability and bound with a spiral binder, two notebook rings, or ribbon threaded through binding holes and tied.

How often should teachers use big books?

Teachers should read each big book to the class several times so that children have the opportunity to remember the words and focus on their printed form. Occasionally a book is so popular that the children may ask to have it read again immediately after the first reading. More often, teachers may repeat the reading of a big book several times over a one- to two-week period, depending on the children's interest. Some teachers may choose to alternate reading a big book with using an interactive chart based on the same book. (See chapter 3 for information on interactive charts.) Although teachers may not wish to use big books every week, they should use them frequently throughout the year.

What should teachers consider when presenting big books to groups of children?

Teachers should consider what specific teaching techniques they wish to use, as well as the seating of the children, when presenting big books to groups. If the children are not yet familiar with the book, teachers may choose to initially read it without pointing to the words in order to familiarize the children with the story. Once children know the book well, the teacher will probably wish to point to the text as he reads. Periodically, teachers may wish to employ a *cloze* technique by pausing at particular points so children can fill in the words. For example, if a book has a rhyming text, the teacher may read the first rhyming word but pause so that the children can think of the second rhyming word.

To benefit from big books, children need to see the text clearly. For this reason, seating becomes important. Many teachers like to use a semicircle seating arrangement at group time. This allows each child an unobstructed view of the teacher. If children are seated too far to the side of the book, however, they will not be able to see it. Teachers can experiment with seating patterns and use carpet squares to designate where each child should sit.

Whenever possible, teachers should have available in the classroom a regular-size version of a book being used in big-book format. Some children may have trouble focusing on the big book during group time and prefer to follow the text in the regular book. When a regular-size version of the big book is available in the book area, children can imitate techniques used by the teacher as they look at the book independently or read it with a friend. Teachers often observe children playing "teacher" and pointing to the words in a book as they conduct their own group time.

How can teachers use big books to encourage phonetic awareness?

Teachers can point out phonetic concepts within the context of the big book and ask questions that encourage children to construct phonetic relationships. Children's first sound–letter associations are typically the initial consonants in words. Teachers can emphasize the sounds of particular letters by selecting words in the story that children recognize and by stressing each word's initial letter and sound. They can then encourage children to think of other words that start with that sound. Since children often remember the initial letters and sounds of their own names and their friends' names, teachers can help children associate the beginning letters and sounds of classmates' names with words in the big book that begin with the same sound.

Teachers should not stop to emphasize phonetic sounds the first time they read a big book, since this might interfere with children's enjoyment and understanding of the story. Comments and questions related to phonics can be interjected on subsequent readings.

What are some other benefits of big books?

Big books can be used to stimulate multicultural awareness, meet the specific needs of individual children, and encourage interest in writing. Children are fascinated with the idea that words look and sound different in various languages. Teachers can construct big books that allow children to say and see specific words in other languages. Activity 2.1 is an example.

Teachers may find that big books are especially helpful for children who have language delays or are learning English as a second language. The repetitive nature of the text combined with the predictable nature of the illustrations helps children learn vocabulary and remember sentence constructions.

As children begin to identify particular words in big books, they may also become interested in writing them. Teachers can encourage this interest by printing the words onto cards and adding them to the class writing center. For example, if a class is reading the big book *The Napping House,* by Audrey Wood, the names of the characters from the book might be included in the writing center. See chapter 5 for more information about writing centers.

How can teachers modify big books for children with specific disabilities?

Depending on the specific needs of individual children, teachers may need to alter the print in big books, choose shorter big books, or read selected portions to some children. Children with visual disabilities may require big books with high contrast between the print and the paper. For these children, black letters on white paper may be easier to see than colored letters. Some children may need to feel the print. In this case, the letters can be traced with puffy paint. For children who are learning braille, teachers can use a braille machine to write the text.

Some children have trouble concentrating on books unless the text is very short. Teachers can vary the length of a big book depending on the individual needs of their class or of particular children. For example, big books made from songs may contain several verses. Teachers may decide to start with just one verse and add other verses later. If the majority of the class is ready to read the entire big book, the teacher may choose to read just a portion of the book to individual children who are not yet able to sit through the whole book.

How can teachers assess children's literacy development through the use of big books?

Teachers can observe children's participation at group time when big books are read, and they can watch for children to use associated materials, such as word cards in the writing center or regular-size versions of the book. Teachers often notice that some of the quieter children in the class eagerly read big books along with the group. They may feel more comfortable participating in a group than individually. Many children are attracted to curriculum materials related to big books that have been shared with the class. Teachers can record their observations on index cards that are filed under each child's name or in a notebook with a section for each child. Anecdotal records can also be included in portfolio assessments.

Big-Book Activities

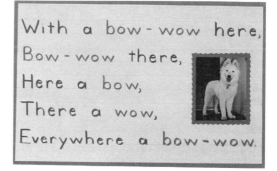

With a bow-wow here,
Bow-wow there,
Here a bow,
There a wow,
Everywhere a bow-wow.

2.1 Hello, Good-Bye

Description

Children are fascinated with the way words look and sound in other languages. This predictable big book introduces "hello" and "good-bye" in many languages through a repeating poem.

> I make new friends the more I grow,
> Did you ever wonder why
> It's much more fun to say "hello"
> Than to have to say "good-bye."
>
> ©2000 Sally Moomaw

Child's Level

This big book is appropriate for preschool and kindergarten children.

Materials

- ◆ 6 pieces of white construction paper, 12 by 18 inches
- ◆ illustrations of children from various cultures, cut from calendars or magazines
- ◆ class picture, for the cover
- ◆ colored sentence strips, with one line of text printed on each page
- ◆ extra lamination film or clear acetate, to form pockets over the words *hello* and *good-bye* (see Helpful Hint)
- ◆ extra pieces of sentence strip, for word cards to put in the pockets

Helpful Hint

Attach the pockets to the big book with clear packing tape after the pages have been laminated.

Language	Word for Hello	Word for Good-bye
Filipino	*mabuhay* (*pronounced* mah-boo-HI)	*paalam* (*pronounced* pah-AH-lahm)
Finnish	*hei* (*pronounced* HEY)	*hei*
Indonesian	*selamat datang* (*pronounced* che-lah-mate dha-thang)	*selamat jalan* (*pronounced* che-lah-mate jah-lane)
Spanish	*hola* (*pronounced* OH-lah)	*adios* (*pronounced* ah-dee-OHS)

What to Look For

Children will read along with the teacher.

Children will quickly learn how to say "hello" and "good-bye" in other languages.

Some children will recognize the language the words are written in after several experiences.

Children will enjoy reading the book to one another and inserting various word cards.

Modification

For young preschoolers, teachers may wish to begin with just one set of word cards from another language. Additional word cards can be used with older children.

Comments & Questions to Extend Thinking

Can you tell what language this word is written in?

Which one of these two words says "hello"?

Find another word for "hello."

Comments & Questions to Encourage Phonetic Awareness

What sound does "hello" start with?

Think of another word that starts with the letter "h."

Integrated Curriculum Activities

Read the book *What Is Your Language?* by Debra Leventhal (New York: Dutton, 1994), to the class. Children can listen for "yes" and "no" in other languages.

Put word cards for *hello* and *good-bye* in various languages in the writing center. Children may be interested in copying them. (See chapter 5.)

2.2 Kitten on the Wall

Description
This poem by William Wordsworth makes an excellent big book.
Children are interested in the topic and can provide the illustrations for the big book. The illustrations and rhyme help children
remember the text.

> See the kitten on the wall,
> Sporting with the leaves that fall,
> Withered leaves—one, two, and three,
> Falling from the elder tree,
> Through the calm and frosty air,
> Of the morning bright and fair.

Helpful Hint

Real leaves can be
substituted for leaf
stickers.

Child's Level
This big book is appropriate for preschool, kindergarten, and first-
grade children.

Materials
- 8 pieces of white construction paper, 12 by 18 inches
- cat illustrations, drawn by the children or cut from a magazine,
  to illustrate each page
- leaf stickers or cutouts
- orange sentence strips, with one line of text printed on
  each page

What to Look For

Children will follow the words as the teacher points to them.

Some children will read along with the teacher.

Some children will read the book to their friends in imitation of the teacher.

Modification

Some children may wish to have their own, smaller copy of the book. The words can be printed on 8½-by-11-inch paper. Children can illustrate their own books.

Comments & Questions to Extend Thinking

Can you find the word "kitten" on this page?

What does the first word say?

Point to a word for a number.

Comments & Questions to Encourage Phonetic Awareness

What sound does "kitten" start with?

Someone in our class has a name that starts with the same sound as "kitten." Can you figure out who that is?

Which word sounds like "wall"?

Integrated Curriculum Activities

Put important words from the big book, such as *kitten* and *leaves,* in the writing center (See chapter 5).

Include other books about kittens, such as *Mama Cat Has Three Kittens,* by Denise Fleming (New York: Holt, 1998), in the reading area.

Take a field trip to a veterinary office.

Transform the dramatic play area into a pet hospital.

2.3 Building Blocks

With our blocks,
Big and small,
We build as we play.

_____ 5u/0 _____ built a

house

With our blocks today.

With our blocks,
Big and small,
We build as we play.

Ben _____ built a

firetruck _____

With our blocks today.

Sally Moomaw
©1997

With our blocks, big and small, We build as we play.

Jen - ny built a cast - le, To - ny built a tow - er,

Nan - cy built a school — With our blocks to - day.

Description
This big book is based on a repetitive song. It allows children to include their names in the song and tell what they like to build with blocks. Children use paper collage pieces cut into the shapes and colors of small wooden blocks to illustrate the pages of the book. Each child can contribute a page. Children are eager to read this class big book again and again. As they listen to the changes made to the text by each child, they increasingly focus on the written words.

Child's Level
This activity is appropriate for older preschool, kindergarten, or first-grade children.

Materials
- white construction paper, 12 by 18 inches (one sheet per child), with the words to the song clearly printed on each sheet and blanks left for the name of each child and what he or she built
- divided tray containing construction-paper collage pieces cut in the shapes and colors of table blocks
- glue containers

What to Look For

Children will quickly memorize the words to the song and follow along as they listen to the big book.

Children will recognize their names in the book and point to the words for the buildings they made.

Many children will learn to read the names of all of the children in the class.

Some children will begin to read words from the book in other contexts.

Children will begin to construct voice–print pairing and left-to-right orientation.

Modification

Older children may wish to draw representations of their block structures rather than glue collage pieces.

Comments & Questions to Extend Thinking

Can you find the word for "blocks" on this page?

Who made this page? How can you tell?

John wrote "skyscraper" on his page. That's a long word.

Comments & Questions to Encourage Phonetic Awareness

This name starts with an "s" like "Sarah," but it's another name. Can you think of someone else whose name starts with an "s"?

Elijah wants to write "house" on his page. What sound do you hear at the beginning of "house"?

What word in the song sounds like "play"?

Integrated Curriculum Activities

Let children help tell the story of *Changes, Changes,* by Pat Hutchins (New York: Macmillan, 1971). Block people assemble a variety of structures with table blocks in this delightful, word-less book.

Include colored table blocks in the manipulative or block areas.

Change the dramatic play area into a construction zone, with hard hats and wooden or plastic tools.

Design math games with a construction theme (see *Much More Than Counting,* activities 6.8, 7.8a, and 7.8b).

Helpful Hints

Trace around table blocks to produce patterns for the collage pieces.

You can print the words on a computer and then adhere them to the construction paper, or simply hand-print them directly onto the paper.

2.4   Class Baby Book

When I was a baby
I looked like this,
Guess who it could be!

Now open the door
and you can see,

It's me!

Description
This big book includes a baby photo and a current photo of each child in the class. The repeating text is perfect for emergent readers, and the photographs motivate children to read the book again and again with their friends.

> When I was a baby I looked like this,
> Guess who it could be!
> Now open the door and you can see,
> It's me!
>
> ©2000 Sally Moomaw

Child's Level
This book is most appropriate for preschool or kindergarten children.

Helpful Hint
Attach the flaps to each page with packing tape after the book has been laminated.

Materials

- construction paper, 12 by 18 inches, one sheet per child, in assorted colors
- computer-generated text, mounted on the construction paper, as pictured
- color copies of each child's baby photo and current photo
- flap, made of laminated construction paper, attached to the book after the book has been laminated to hide the child's current photo (see Helpful Hint)

What to Look For

Children will eagerly guess the identities of the babies in the photos.

Children will read along with the teacher, following the left-to-right progression and voice–print pairing.

Children will return to the book to read it on their own.

Modification

For very young children, limit the text to the word *baby* printed next to the baby picture and the child's name below the current picture.

Comments & Questions to Extend Thinking

Who do you think this baby is?

Can you find the word for "baby" on this page?

Look at the word "I." It's a letter and a word!

Comments & Questions to Encourage Phonetic Awareness

Which words end with an "ee" sound in this book?

Listen for the sound that "baby" begins with. What letter makes that sound?

Whose picture is this? If we wrote her name, what letter would it start with?

Integrated Curriculum Activities

Explore other identity activities, such as making hand and foot prints (see *More Than Painting,* activities 5.24 and 8.5).

Create math games with a baby theme (see *Much More Than Counting,* activities 1.16, 6.9, 7.9a, and 7.9b).

Sing songs about babies (see *More Than Singing,* activities 2.1, 2.9, 2.12, and 2.13).

 **The Arlitt* Mail Book**

** Substitute the name of your school for "Arlitt,"
which is the name of our school.*

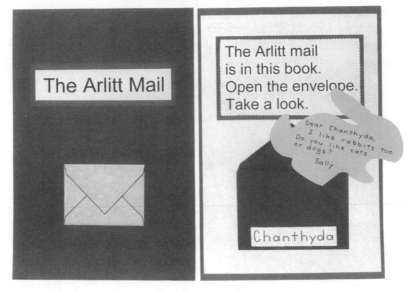

Description

This big book includes a special page for each child with an envelope and a note from the teacher. The children's messages can be changed whenever desired. Children learn to read the poem, which appears on every page, as well as their own messages.

> The Arlitt mail is in this book.
> Open the envelope. Take a look.

Child's Level

This book is appropriate for preschool, kindergarten, and first-grade children. The length and content of the messages can be altered depending on the age and development of the children.

Materials

- white construction paper, 12 by 18 inches, one sheet per child, with the poem printed on it
- 1 large colored envelope per page, with a different child's name printed on each envelope
- 2 pieces of dark blue construction paper, for the front and back covers, with the book title and an envelope mounted to the front
- message for each child, to include in the envelopes

Laminate the envelopes before attaching them to the book pages. Write the children's names in permanent marker over the lamination. The permanent marker can be removed with alcohol and the book reused in subsequent years.

The envelopes can be slit open after they are laminated.

Be sure to print the messages clearly so that emergent readers can read them.

What to Look For

Children will eagerly open their envelopes to see the messages.

Children will quickly remember the predictable text that accompanies each page.

Some children may wish to add messages of their own to the big book.

Modification

Include brief messages for younger children and longer and more complex messages for older children.

Comments & Questions to Extend Thinking

Whose message is in this envelope?

This is a message for Karen. Can you help me find her envelope?

Do you remember what your message says? Let's look at it together.

Comments & Questions to Encourage Phonetic Awareness

Can you find a word that looks and sounds like this word—"look"?

Jeff's name starts with a "j." Can you think of another name that starts with that sound?

Integrated Curriculum Activities

Set up a post office in the dramatic play area with a mailbox for each child.

Read books about mail, such as *A Letter to Amy*, by Ezra Jack Keats (New York: Harper & Row, 1968).

Include envelopes in the writing center to encourage children to write messages.

Send home a post office literary suitcase (activity 8.5).

2.6 Hush Little Baby

Description

This classic Appalachian lullaby makes an excellent text for a big book. Children quickly remember the predictable text and like to read or sing along.

Traditional

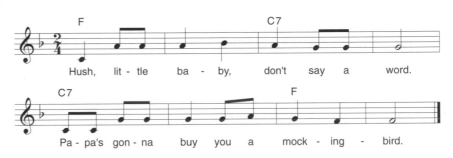

Hush, little baby, don't say a word,
Papa's gonna buy you a mockingbird.

If that mockingbird won't sing,
Papa's gonna buy you a diamond ring.

If that diamond ring turns brass,
Papa's gonna buy you a looking glass.

If that looking glass gets broke,
Papa's gonna buy you a billy goat.

If that billy goat won't pull,
Papa's gonna buy you a cart and bull.

If that cart and bull turn over,
Papa's gonna buy you a dog named Rover.

If that dog named Rover won't bark,
Papa's gonna buy you a horse and cart.

If that horse and cart fall down,
You'll still be the sweetest little baby in town.

Child's Level

This book is appropriate for older preschool, kindergarten, and first-grade children.

Materials

- white construction paper, 12 by 18 inches
- baby pictures cut from magazines, for the illustrations
- stickers or drawings of the presents Papa brings to baby, for the illustrations
- colored sentence strips, with one line of text printed on each page

What to Look For

Children will quickly read or sing along, using the illustrations as clues.

Children will follow the left-to-right progression of the text.

Children will fill in the rhyming words if the teacher pauses to give them time.

Modification

Older children may wish to create additional verses for the song.

Comments & Questions to Extend Thinking

What would you bring for baby?

Look at the word for "Papa." Can you find "Papa" on this page?

Comments & Questions to Encourage Phonetic Awareness

Which word sounds like "sing"? Are any of the letters the same?

Listen to the sound of the "sh" at the end of "hush." It's just like the "sh" at the end of "fish."

What sounds do you hear in the word "baby"?

Integrated Curriculum Activities

Put rattles made of different materials in the music area (see *More Than Magnets*, activity 6.13).

Include word cards with baby toys in the writing area. Children may wish to write their own baby books.

Read other books about babies, such as *Hush!* by Minfong Ho (New York: Orchard Books, 1996), and *Sleep, Sleep, Sleep*, by Nancy Van Laan (Boston: Little, Brown, 1995).

Helpful Hint

You can also use photographs of baby toys cut from catalogs instead of stickers for the illustrations.

Description
This teacher-made mystery book includes clues for each hidden picture and a tiny window through which to peek at just a portion of the picture.

Child's Level
This book is most appropriate for preschool or kindergarten children.

Materials
- colored construction paper, 12 by 18 inches, with a small square cut in every other page to form a window
- pictures of animals or familiar objects, cut from magazines and mounted to the pieces of construction paper that do not have windows (each picture should be visible through the window of the page before it)
- black marker, to print several clues on each page, followed by the sentence "What is it?"

What to Look For
Children will read the repeated phrase on each page along with the teacher.

Children will guess what the pictures are.

Some children will base their guesses on the clues, while others will guess solely on the appearance of the picture.

Some children will help read the clues.

Helpful Hint
Decide on the placement and size of the windows after the illustrations have been mounted.

Modification

Write simple, one-word clues for young children.

Comments & Questions to Extend Thinking

This word says "big." Did we see that word on any other page?
What animal could be furry *and* white?

Comments & Questions to Encourage Phonetic Awareness

Listen to the sound the "wh" makes in "what." Can you think of
   any other words that start with that sound?
Help me read this clue. It starts with a "buh" sound.

Integrated Curriculum Activities

Read other books that encourage children to look carefully at pic-
   tures, such as *Look, Look, Look,* by Tana Hoban (New York:
   Greenwillow, 1988).
Play guessing games with the children, perhaps during lunch.
   They can think up clues for the object they are thinking of.
Let children create their own guessing books. Make blank books
   with windows cut out of every other page. Children can glue or
   draw pictures under the windows and write clues.

2.8 A-Hunting We Will Go

Description

This traditional rhyming song makes an excellent big book.
Children can make up additional rhymes and illustrate the pages.
Singing the words encourages many children to join in when they
might not participate otherwise.

Child's Level

This book is most appropriate for older preschool, kindergarten,
or first-grade children.

Repeating Verse	Example
Oh, a-hunting we will go,	Oh, a-hunting we will go,
A-hunting we will go,	A-hunting we will go,
We'll catch a _____	We'll catch a <u>kitten</u>,
And put it in a _____	And put it in a <u>mitten</u>,
And then we'll let it go.	And then we'll let it go.

Materials

◆ pastel construction paper, 12 by 18 inches, with the words clearly printed on each page, as pictured
◆ drawings or cutouts, for the initial illustrations
◆ markers, for the children's illustrations

What to Look For

Children will read or sing along with the teacher almost immediately because the repeating text is so easy to remember.
Children will delight in filling in the rhyming words.
Some children will begin to make up their own rhyming words.
Some children will compare the way the rhyming words look.
Some children will focus on reading the rhyming words, especially if they are printed in a different color.

Modifications

For young children, start with just four or five verses.
Older children may wish to add many additional verses to the song.

Comments & Questions to Extend Thinking

What does this word say (pointing to "Oh")?
We'll catch a "kitten," and put it in a _____ (long pause, so that children can focus on and fill in the rhyming word).
Do you see this word ("a-hunting") anywhere else on the page?
What would you like to catch, Kevin? What would rhyme with that?

Comments & Questions to Encourage Phonetic Awareness

"Kitten" and "mitten" almost sound the same, except for the beginning. (Say the two words deliberately.)
What sound does "kitten" start with? What letter makes that sound?
What sound does "mitten" start with? What letter makes that sound?
I want to catch a "bunny." What would rhyme with that?

Integrated Curriculum Activities

Add word cards with the rhyming words to the writing center (activity 5.14).
Make individual books for the children on smaller-size paper. They can fill in the rhyming words and illustrate their own books.
Read other animal books with a predictable text, such as *Dear Zoo,* by Rod Campbell (Washington, DC: Four Winds, 1982).

Helpful Hint

Children can draw the illustrations on separate sheets of paper. They can then be cut out and mounted to the book pages without disturbing the print.

2.9 Silly Friends

Silly Peter played bells
at school,
Upside down, looking cool.

Description

This book incorporates upside-down pictures of each child in the classroom. The text repeats, with a different name and verb on each page, depending on the photo. Children delight in the silliness and eagerly look to see what each of their friends is doing in the book.

Silly <u>Molly</u> <u>painted</u> at school,
Upside down, looking cool.

Child's Level

This book is most appropriate for preschool or kindergarten children.

Materials

- story paper, 12 by 18 inches (lined on half of the page and blank on the other half)
- colored construction paper, 12 by 18 inches, to mount the story paper on (for color contrast and durability)
- photo of each child in the class doing something at school, mounted upside down on the page

Helpful Hint

Trim ¼ inch from each side of the story paper before starting. This will allow a border of color to show when it is mounted on construction paper.

What to Look For

Children will look for their own photos and the photos of their classmates, and then look at how the names are written.

Children will listen for the changing verb on each page, and then look to see how it is written.

Children will read the book along with the teacher.

Children will read the book to one another and correct each other's mistakes.

Modification

For younger children, use a contrasting color to write the children's names and the words that describe their actions. This helps them focus on particular words and realign their voice–print pairing.

Comments & Questions to Extend Thinking

Whose name is on this page? What letter does it start with?

Look at Danny's picture. Can you guess what this word (point to the verb) says he did?

Comments & Questions to Encourage Phonetic Awareness

What word sounds like "school"?

Look at the words "school" and "cool." Does anything look the same?

Maria's name starts with an "mm" sound. Are there any other names in our class that start with that sound?

Integrated Curriculum Activities

Read *Silly Sally*, by Audrey Wood (New York: Harcourt, 1992). Children enjoy the rhyme and the upside-down characters.

Make path games with upside-down counters or movers (see *Much More Than Counting*, activities 5.14, 6.1, 7.1a, 7.1b, and 8.8).

Plan upside-down gross-motor activities, such as wheelbarrow walks. The teacher holds the children's feet so they can walk on their hands, which increases upper body strength.

2.10 Old MacDonald

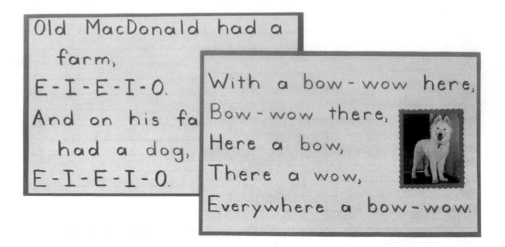

Old MacDonald had a farm,
E-I-E-I-O.
And on his fa[rm he] had a dog,
E-I-E-I-O.

With a bow-wow here,
Bow-wow there,
Here a bow,
There a wow,
Everywhere a bow-wow.

Description

Familiar songs, such as "Old MacDonald," translate well into big-book format when the text repeats, with small changes in each verse. Since children often already know the words, they can quickly begin to follow the print as the teacher points. Children love to sing along.

Child's Level

This book is most appropriate for preschool or kindergarten children.

Traditional

Old Mac-Don-ald had a farm, E-I-E-I-O, And on his farm he had a dog, E-I-E-I-O, With a bow-wow here and a bow-wow there, Here a bow, there a wow, ev-ery-where a bow-wow, Old Mac-Don-ald had a farm, E-I-E-I-O.

Materials
- chart paper (lined flip-chart-size paper), cut to 12 by 18 inches
- colored construction paper, 12 by 18 inches, to mount the chart paper on (for color contrast and durability)
- animal illustrations, cut from magazines or coloring books
- black marker, to print the words
- colored marker, to print the name of each animal and the sound it makes

What to Look For
Many children will remember the words to the song and quickly sing along.

Children will focus on the repeating words, such as the sounds the animals make, and notice that they look alike.

Some children will remember the spellings of some of the animals, such as *cow* or *pig*.

Modification
Start with just a few animals for very young children.

Comments & Questions to Extend Thinking
What sound does the cow make? Do you see that word anywhere?

Find two words that look the same. Let's see if they sound the same in the song. (For example, "moo, moo.")

"And on his farm he had a _____." (Pause, so that the children can fill in the word.)

Comments & Questions to Encourage Phonetic Awareness
If we put the word "horse" in the song, what sound would it start with?

This animal starts with a "p." (Make the sound several times before reading the word.)

What sound does the "m" make in "moo"?

Integrated Curriculum Activities
Read other books about farm animals, such as *The Very Busy Spider,* by Eric Carle (New York: Philomel, 1984).

Create a farm animal math game (see *Much More Than Counting,* activities 6.4, 7.4a, 7.4b, and 8.9).

Take a field trip to a farm. Let children vote on their favorite farm animals and graph the results (see *More Than Counting,* chapter 6).

Put word cards of the animals from "Old MacDonald" in the writing area (see chapter 5 for information about writing centers).

Helpful Hint
Use a contrasting color of marker for the names of the animals and their sounds. This helps children reorient themselves with voice–print pairing.

2.11 Rain, Rain, Go Away

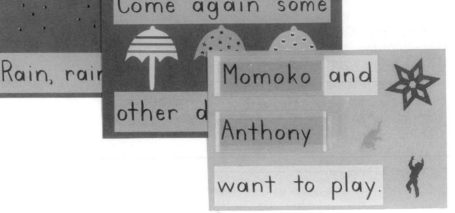

Traditional

Rain, rain, go a - way,

Come a - gain some oth - er day,

We want to go out and play.

Description
This big book adds the names of all of the children in the class to a familiar children's song. Two clear pockets on the last page allow children to change the names in the song.

Rain, rain, go away,
Come again some other day,
_____ and _____ want to play.

Child's Level
This book is appropriate for preschool and kindergarten children.

Materials
- 4 pieces of dark blue construction paper, 12 by 18 inches each, for the first and second pages of text and the front and back covers
- 1 piece of yellow construction paper, for the third page of text
- cloud cutouts and rain stickers, for the illustration on the first page
- umbrella cutouts, for the illustration on the second page
- sun cutout and child-silhouette stickers, for the illustration on the last page

- blue sentence strips, to print the first and second lines of text on
- yellow sentence strip, to print the third line of text on
- extra laminating film, to form two clear pockets on the final page
- blue sentence strips or index cards, for the children's names

What to Look For

Children will sing the song as the teacher points to the words.

Children will be very interested in how the name cards change the way the last line is read.

Many children will read and sing the book with one another, changing the names on the last page each time.

Children will correct one another if the names are not read accurately.

Modification

For very young preschoolers, put only one pocket on the final page and add just one name at a time.

Comments & Questions to Extend Thinking

How many times do you see the word "rain"?

I want to put Nicole's name in the song. What letter should I look for at the beginning of her name?

What does the last line say now?

Comments & Questions to Encourage Phonetic Awareness

Look at how the word "away" ends, with an "ay." Does any other word in the song end with that sound?

What sound does this name start with?

Can you think of two names that start with the same sound?

Integrated Curriculum Activities

Read other books about rainy days, such as *The Napping House*, by Audrey Wood (New York: Harcourt, 1984).

Sing other songs about rain, and add instruments to create the rain sounds (see *More Than Singing*, activities 2.10, 3.14, 3.15, 4.13, 4.14, and 4.15).

Put rainsticks in the music area (see *More Than Singing*, activity 5.6).

Make pictures with eye droppers and colored water.

Helpful Hint

Attach the pockets with clear packing tape after the book pages have been laminated.

CHAPTER 3

Interactive Charts

Bowen entered a child care program at age three. He had been in the United States only two months, and his parents expressed concerns about his ability to play with the other children. Bowen listened during group time each day as the teacher sang "Look Who's Here." The teacher placed a child's name in each blank space on a chart that read "Look who's here, it's _____. Look who's here, it's _____. They are all at school today." Within five days Bowen read his name and the names of several other children as the teacher showed the name cards. Subsequently, he pretended that he was the teacher leading group as he held up each name card and looked at the specific child.

▲ ▲ ▲

Bonnie ran to meet her mother and third-grade sister at departure time. "Mom! Hurry. I can read just like Megan." Bonnie led her mother and sister to the chart hanging on the wall near the book area. The chart included the familiar words to Bonnie's favorite book, Brown Bear, Brown Bear, What Do You See? *by Bill Martin Jr. As she read the predictable text, Bonnie pointed to each word. She had constructed important information about reading. She knew that every written word represented a word she read.*

▲ ▲ ▲

Children are surrounded by print every day. They are especially interested in interactive charts, which can be included in the reading area, music center, dramatic play area, or other curriculum centers in early childhood classrooms. The charts provide opportunities for children to observe enlarged print, recognize letters and words, and change the meaning of the text through manipulation of key words. Many children construct reading concepts and demonstrate reading behaviors associated with emergent readers as they explore interactive charts.

Teachers' Questions

What are interactive charts?

Interactive charts are enlarged-print versions of poems, songs, or other predictable text. The charts include one or more opportunities for children to change key-word cards and thus alter the meaning of the text. The design of these charts encourages children to interact with print in meaningful ways. Many preschool and kindergarten teachers sing songs that include the names of children. For example, the teacher might sing "Look who's here, it's _____," adding a child's name as she sings each stanza. To incorporate this song into an interactive-chart activity, the teacher could print the words of the song on poster board and leave a blank at the end of the sentence. Children quickly recognize the chart as the printed version of the song. They eagerly wait for their names to be included in the song and just as eagerly wait to see their names in print as they are added to the chart in the blank space. The activities in this chapter use examples of charts that include children's names or other high-interest words as interactive pieces.

How did interactive charts evolve as part of the literacy curriculum?

Interactive charts evolved from early attempts to include meaningful print in the curriculum. The first charts made by teachers at our center were enlarged-print versions of poems and songs. Children matched separate word cards to words on the chart. For example, children might match word cards such as *one, two, three,* and *four* to the same words in a simple number song. As we observed children interacting with the materials, however, we realized that while they were interested in the print, that interest was not sustained, and the knowledge of isolated words did not appear to enhance children's understanding of reading or writing. Since the most meaningful written words for children are their names, we began to use children's names as the key words to manipulate on the charts. This was more than mere matching. Children recognized that changing one word changed the meaning of the print. The result of our early explorations is the interactive chart.

Why are interactive charts important to include in the early childhood classroom?

Interactive charts provide opportunities for children to engage in activities with meaningful print and develop a solid knowledge base about reading. As children observe the print of interactive charts and manipulate key words, they construct knowledge about letters and words, create relationships between the spoken word and the written word, develop phonetic awareness, and develop confidence as emergent readers. The enlarged print of the charts allows children to more easily recognize, discriminate, match, and compare letters and words. The enlarged print clearly delineates word boundaries so that children more readily associate one spoken word with one written word and create sound–symbol relationships. These relationships are valuable as children become independent readers. Children also have more control over the meaning of the print as they change one or more key words of the text.

Some interactive charts encourage children to construct information about writing. In some cases teachers provide opportunities for children to suggest the key words to change on a chart. Children can write their suggestions on paper to add to the chart. This encourages children to engage in emergent writing experiences. Activity 3.10 is an example of an interactive chart that encourages children to write their suggestions.

At what age do children benefit from experiences using interactive charts?

Preschool, kindergarten, and first-grade children benefit from explorations with interactive charts. In some cases children as young as two and a half years old may also benefit from experiences interacting with the print on the charts. Kindergarten and first-grade teachers may find interactive charts useful in teaching orthographic features, such as punctuation and capitalization. The enlarged text makes these print features more noticeable for some children.

What materials are needed to make interactive charts?

Poster board, sentence strips, markers, and adhesive are needed to make interactive charts. These supplies are available through school-supply catalogs. Poster board is sold in a wide variety of colors. Sentence strips are available in white, manila, and pastel colors. Watercolor markers with pointed tips rather than flat tips are the best for reproducing large manuscript letters. Permanent markers bleed through the strips and generally make a line that is too thin for the size of the print. Teachers who print left-handed may want to use a permanent marker, however. Watercolor markers may smudge as the left hand touches the letters already formed.

The charts must be laminated to make them durable for use with children. Many school districts, teacher-resource centers, and copy services laminate materials such as interactive charts. Although a clear self-adhesive covering such as Con-Tact can be used, it is difficult to adhere it to large charts, and it often wrinkles or bubbles. This makes the chart less attractive and may also obscure the print.

How do teachers decide what color combinations to select when designing interactive charts?

Teachers should select colors to coordinate with the topic of the chart, the color of sentence strips and marker, and the illustration. Charts based on a predictable book should also coordinate with the colors of the book. For example, an interactive chart based on *It Looked Like Spilt Milk* should be made using dark blue poster board to match the color of the book pages. Teachers might use a brown marker and manila sentence strips on brown poster board for a bakery song and pastel strips on white poster board for a lullaby. Black poster board, white sentence strips, and black marker are safe choices for many charts. Teachers should avoid fluorescent poster board, which may appear too bright and is difficult to coordinate with most illustrations. Yellow marker is too light for children to read on the charts. Many examples of color combinations are given in the individual activities.

How can teachers assemble interactive charts?

The easiest way for teachers to create interactive charts is to print the words to a song, poem, or other predictable text on sentence strips, attach the strips to poster board, and add an appropriate picture cue. Teachers should use a standard manuscript form as the model for the print. An example of an appropriate alphabet model is included in appendix B. Some teachers use a ruler to make the straight lines. The sentence strips and an appropriate illustration can be attached to the poster board with a glue stick, rubber cement, or spray adhesive.

What should teachers avoid when designing interactive charts?

Teachers should avoid nonstandard letter formation, inconsistency in size and formation of letters, and inadequate spacing between letters and words. Attention to details such as these ensures that charts are attractive, model appropriate letter formation, and provide opportunities for children to distinguish individual letters and words, compare upper and lowercase letters, and readily perceive word boundaries.

How do children associate an interactive chart with a particular poem, song, or predictable book?

Children associate the words on an interactive chart with a specific poem, song, or predictable book because of context cues included as part of the design of the interactive chart. Teachers should include appropriate picture cues in the design of each interactive chart. The pictures give nonreaders a context for predicting the meaning of the print. For example, the teacher might use snowflake cutouts to decorate the interactive chart for the song "Snowflakes Are Swirling" (activity 3.3) or insect stickers to decorate the chart for the chant "I Went Camping" (activity 3.5).

What criteria should teachers consider when selecting a poem or song for an interactive chart?

Teachers should consider
- *the interests of the children*
- *the length of the poem or song*
- *the repetitiveness of the words*
- *the content or subject matter of the poem or song*
- *the specific literacy goals*
- *how the poem or song connects to other curricular activities*

How long should the poems or songs be?

In general, poems and songs should be four to six lines long. This length is appropriate for most interactive chart selections; however, younger or less experienced children may benefit from one- and two-line poems or songs transferred to interactive charts.

Why is the repetition of words important?

Young children love repetition, and poems or songs with repetitive words are easier for them to learn and remember. Children more easily associate each spoken word with the print on the charts when they accurately remember the text, word for word.

What constitutes appropriate content for poems and songs?

The content of poems and songs should be relevant to the children's lives. Songs and poems about children and families, farm and zoo animals, the weather, and classroom activities are appropriate because these are topics familiar to children. For example, the poem "Scarf Dancing" (activity 3.8) appeals to children who have had experiences dancing with scarves at group time and in the dramatic play area. Likewise, children are drawn to "The Mitten" poem chart (activity 3.4) when they are interested in the book based on the Ukrainian folktale.

What should teachers avoid when selecting poems and songs for interactive charts?

Teachers should avoid text longer than six lines, text that incorporates numbers, text with potential subject/verb conflict, and text with gender-specific pronouns. The traditional song "Five Little Ducks" is appropriate to include in the music curriculum of early childhood programs. Yet attempts to make this song into an interactive chart pose potential problems. Printing all the verses of the song makes it too long to fit on six sentence strips; however, printing a single verse of the song as an interactive chart would look like the example below. The problem occurs as children place the number words in the blank spaces. Imagine that a child places the word card *two* in the first blank and the word card *one* in the last blank. Read the words out loud and the grammatical error is apparent.

> ____ little ducks went out to play
> Over the hills and far away.
> Mother duck said, "Quack, quack, quack!"
> ____ little ducks came waddling back.

The traditional song "Oh, A-Hunting We Will Go" is also appropriate to include in the music curriculum, yet it doesn't work as an interactive chart. The problems associated with this song relate to gender. The chart could look like the example below.

> Oh a-hunting <u>Charlie</u> will go
> He'll catch a fox and put him in a box
> And then he'll let him go.

Replace the name "Charlie" with "Bonnie" and the gender issue is apparent.

What should teachers consider when selecting part of a book to use as an interactive chart?

Teachers should select a specific sentence, which repeats throughout the text of the book. Some books, such as *It Looked Like Spilt Milk*, by Charles G. Shaw, have a repetitive structure. The text on each page is exactly the same with the exception of one word. "Sometimes it looked like _____. But it wasn't _____." Children quickly recognize the pattern of the written language. They are able to change the meaning of the text by selecting word cards to place in the blanks on the chart. Other books, such as

Owl Babies, by Martin Wadell, include a sentence that repeats on almost every page. Since children identify with the smallest owl, Bill, an appropriate text for an interactive chart might be, *"I want my mommy," said Bill.* Children could substitute their names for *Bill.*

What key words are the most important for children to manipulate on the interactive chart?

Teachers should begin with the most important written words for young children—their names. Characters from predictable books or color words are also high-interest words for children to manipulate as they interact with print. Since children are so interested in seeing their names in print, the first charts teachers introduce should incorporate children's names as the interactive words. Throughout the year, teachers should carefully select songs, poems, and text from predictable books that include high-interest words, such as color words, animal names, and the names of the characters in books. These make the best key words for interactive charts.

What are name cards and word cards?

Name cards are enlarged-print versions of the names of the children and teachers in the class. The teacher can print the names on six-to-eight-inch-long sentence strips, which are available in white, manila, and pastel colors and can be purchased through many school-supply catalogs or stores. The strips are already printed with lines that allow teachers to make letters that are consistent in size. Specialty name cards, with decorations such as apples, are also available through some school-supply catalogs. For durability, name cards should be laminated or covered with clear self-adhesive covering such as Con-Tact.

Word cards are enlarged-print versions of high-interest words printed on a variety of index cards or sentence strips. The teacher should select the words based on the children's interests. The words selected are usually nouns, or in the case of color words, adjectives. Teachers should avoid selecting words that are difficult to illustrate on the word cards, such as *windy, big,* and *happy.* An appropriate possibility might be the names of characters from high-interest books, such as *worm, bird, cat,* and *dog* from *The Big Fat Worm,* by Nancy Van Laan. Another possibility might be the names of materials used in dramatic play, such as *hammer, saw,* and *pliers,* or clothing items, such as *hat, mitten,* and *boots.* Some teachers use commercial sentence strips for word cards, while others print the words on small index cards. The word cards should be laminated or covered with clear self-adhesive covering for durability.

Can preschool and kindergarten children read name and word cards?

Young children quickly recognize their names or at least the first letters of their names. Print-rich early childhood classrooms use the children's names in a variety of situations, including on their cubbies, above coat hooks, or on individual boxes for collecting each child's papers. This exposure to their names in print, coupled with high interest in this important label, ensures that children focus on their names. In the past, educators assumed young children could not recognize their names until they could read. Teachers often used a symbol, such as an apple or a carrot, next to the child's name. However, our observations over many years have shown that children do not need such abstract symbols. If in a few isolated cases children do not demonstrate interest in print, including their own names, teachers may choose to mount a small photograph of the child on the name card to generate interest. At a later date, the cards can be remade without the photograph.

Children read other types of word cards because the teacher includes a picture cue next to the printed word. The picture cue provides children with a context for predicting what the print says. Sometimes teachers of older preschool and kindergarten children place the picture cue on the back of the card. This allows emergent readers to verify their ability to read the word. The picture cues selected for the word cards must closely match the word. For example, the teacher might use a rubber stamp of a mitten or a sticker of a hammer for those particular word cards. When book characters are used on word cards, teachers should use the exact illustration from the book whenever possible. Some authors, including Jan Brett and Audrey Wood, have Web sites that encourage teachers to download the illustrations from their books for use in the classroom. Since it is impossible to find an accurate picture cue for body parts, feelings, and descriptive words, such as *big* and *little,* teachers should avoid using those words on word cards. A child might read the word *face* as "head," *rain* as "raining," *big* as "elephant," and *sad* as "unhappy."

Can teachers use the computer to generate the print for name cards?

The computer can be used for name cards and word cards; however, teachers must carefully select the font and size of the print. The most common concerns for teachers using computer-generated print are nonstandard letter formations, such as *a* and *g,* a lack of sufficient differences between letters, as in *a/d* or *h/n,* and insufficient space between letters. In some cases, the computer letters almost touch each other, thus inhibiting children from discriminating one letter from another.

Why should teachers coordinate interactive charts with other curricular materials?

Teachers should coordinate interactive charts with other curricular materials to stimulate interest in the charts, create opportunities for repeated experiences with the same or similar materials, and encourage children to explore related activities. For example, the teacher might place the pizza chart (activity 3.9) in the dramatic play area. The key words are various pizza toppings. The chart may become part of the play as children take orders for pizza from the customers. The chart may also generate interest in an upcoming field trip to a pizza restaurant and a graphing activity of favorite pizza toppings. Pizza-topping word cards (activity 5.8) could also be placed at the writing center, thus providing opportunities for children to interact with the same print in different areas of the classroom.

How often should interactive charts be used in the classroom?

Interactive charts should be a permanent part of the curricular materials in the classroom. One or more interactive charts should be included in the classroom at all times throughout the year.

How long should a specific interactive chart be displayed in the classroom?

Interactive charts, like other curricular materials, should be displayed for an extended period of time, perhaps two to three weeks. Children need opportunities to return to an interactive chart many times in order to construct information about reading and writing. Just as children benefit from repeated experiences with books, math games, and science materials, they also benefit from repeated experiences with each interactive chart. Children pay closer attention to details of individual letters and words, notice word boundaries, and create letter and sound relationships when they have extensive opportunities to interact with the print on the charts.

Where can teachers display interactive charts?

Teachers can display interactive charts in the book, music, dramatic play, and science areas. Since many interactive charts are based on poems and songs, these charts can be displayed in the music area or the dramatic play area when appropriate. Some interactive charts, such as "The Train" (activity 3.2), can be placed in the block area. Interactive charts based on the text from predictable books should be displayed in the book area whenever possible. Teachers may have to be creative in order to make space for interactive charts!

How can interactive charts be displayed in the classroom?

Teachers can use staples or thumbtacks to secure interactive charts to the wall. Most early childhood classrooms have adequate wall space for the display of interactive charts. Teachers should be careful to monitor charts secured by thumbtacks, which may become dislodged from the wall and pose a safety threat. Upholstery tacks are longer and may prevent the charts from coming off the walls as easily.

Teachers can also secure cup hooks in the wall and use bulldog clips to hang the interactive charts from the cup hooks. Mount a strip of wood on the wall before screwing in the cup hooks, or place the cup hook so that it goes into a stud in the wall. See photo to the side for an example of how to use the cup hooks and bulldog clips.

What literacy concepts emerge as children use interactive charts?

Children construct literacy concepts related to reading and writing. Interactive charts provide repeated opportunities for children to see spoken words in written form and thus construct the relationship between oral and written language. They realize that print says the same thing no matter who reads it, how much time elapses, or where the print is located. Children observe the left-to-right and top-to-bottom progression of the text, notice the configuration of words, recognize the function of letters in the formation of words, and make sound–letter associations. Eventually children begin to recognize upper- and lowercase letters, recognize some words, and transition into conventional reading.

Some interactive charts encourage children to supply the words to complete the interactive portion of the chart. For example, children may suggest pizza toppings to add to a chart (activity 3.9). Younger children can dictate ideas for the teacher to write, while older children can write the words themselves.

How do interactive charts help children construct concepts about reading?

The predictable qualities of interactive charts help children construct reading concepts. Pattern is an important component of the language of poems, songs, and predictable books, which have a strong rhyme, rhythm, or repetition. Children readily perceive the pattern and remember the words to such poems, songs, and books. Interactive charts encourage children to read by guessing what the words say based on language patterns they recognize. They are usually correct! Although they may have memorized poems, songs, and books, many children transition into conventional reading as they explore interactive charts and correlate written words with the text they remember.

How can teachers use interactive charts to model reading concepts and behaviors?

Teachers can take advantage of opportunities at group time and throughout the day to model reading concepts and behaviors. Teachers model voice–print pairing by pointing to the words one at a time as they read them. They also draw attention to the predictability of the written language when they use the *cloze* technique, pausing to allow children to fill in an important word in the sentence. For example, the teacher might wait for children to fill in the rhyming word in a poem or song. Teachers can also point out similarities and differences in letters and words. Most young children are interested in the letters of their names and delight in searching for and finding those important letters.

How do interactive charts help children develop concepts about writing?

Charts that provide opportunities for children to write the interactive words help them develop concepts about writing. Teachers can plan specific charts that encourage children to add their suggestions. For example, children can add their own words to the chart "I Went Camping" (activity 3.5). On the one hand, when teachers accept all stages of writing as children add words to charts, they help children become more confident writers. On the other hand, listening to other children attempt to read the words they have added to charts helps older children evaluate their writing. Kindergarten and first-grade children may need to set aside their egocentric views and consider the viewpoint of the reader.

Can other children read nonconventional spelling? Does the reader know that the written word continues on the other side of the paper? These questions may encourage children to pay closer attention to conventional letter formation, spacing between letters and words, and spelling.

How can teachers use interactive charts to model writing concepts and strategies?

Teachers can take advantage of opportunities to model conventional letter formation and spelling. For example, teachers may talk out loud as they write individual letters. This gives children information about how to form certain letters. Teachers can also demonstrate problem-solving strategies related to spelling. For example, teachers can model the use of classroom resources, such as a picture dictionary or environmental print (*open, closed, stop,* or *exit* signs, for example), to help them spell words.

How can teachers modify interactive charts for children with specific disabilities?

Teachers should select shorter text, one or two lines, for charts to use with children who have cognitive delays. Puffy paints can be used to outline the print on charts for children with visual disabilities. Teachers can use a braille machine to write the words for a chart and glue them above the conventional print. Some children with a visual disability benefit from high contrast between the print and the background. Teachers can use black marker on bright yellow sentence strips for very high contrast.

How can teachers use interactive charts to assess children's literacy development?

Teachers can observe children at group time and during children's independent use of interactive charts in the classroom. They may note whether children demonstrate left-to-right and top-to-bottom orientation, voice–print pairing, or recognition of specific words. Some charts encourage children to experiment with writing. Teachers may observe the child's individual stage in the development of writing. Observations may be recorded on index cards collected for each child or in a notebook for each child. Some teachers keep these anecdotal records as part of the child's portfolio with other information and artifacts. Some teachers may use checklists to document the child's progress in literacy development. See appendix C for a reading-assessment checklist and appendix D for a writing-assessment checklist.

Interactive-Chart Activities

I looked in the engine
And what did I see?
I saw Christopher
Looking back at me.

3.1   Look Who's Here

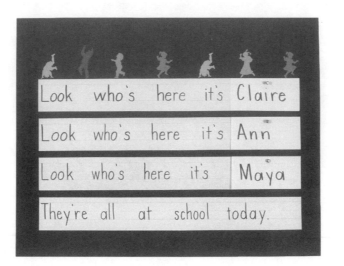

To the tune of "Mary Had a Little Lamb"   ©2000 Brenda Hieronymus

Look who's here, it's Jon-a-than,   Look who's here, it's Ma-ry Ann,

Look who's here, it's Er-ic-a, They're all at school to-day.

Description

Children are very interested in their names and the names of other children. This repetitive song gives them many opportunities to see the names in print. Teachers can use this interactive chart at group time to introduce children to each other during the first days and weeks of school. Later the chart can be placed in the classroom for further exploration.

Child's Level

This chart is appropriate for preschool and kindergarten children.

Materials

- ◆ black poster board
- ◆ white sentence strips
- ◆ black marker
- ◆ silhouette stickers, to decorate the chart
- ◆ paper fastener, ¾ inch
- ◆ name card for each child and teacher in the class, made from white sentence strip, and laminated or covered with clear self-adhesive paper (the name cards should be cut to the exact size of the blank on the chart)

What to Look For

Children will eagerly look for and recognize their own names as
    they sing the song and add names to the chart.
Many children will also look for and recognize the names of others.
Some children may recognize their names by the first letter only.
    These children may select any name card that begins with
    that letter.
Some children will comment on the words that are the same in
    the song.

Modification

Teachers of kindergarten and first-grade children may wish to
    include both the first and last names of the children.

Comments & Questions to Extend Thinking

Whose name should we add to the chart?
Who is here today? Would you like to find their names to add
    to the chart?
I see another name that begins with the same first letter as
    your name.
Casey and Brandy both end with the letter "y."

Comments & Questions to Encourage Phonetic Awareness

Does anyone else have a name that ends with the letter "e"? Does
    it sound the same as Molly and Jamie?
Ciara's name starts with the name for the first letter, "c."
Molly and Jamie both sound like they end with the "e," but Molly
    really ends with the letter "y."

Integrated Curriculum Activities

Include the names of the class on word cards at the writing center.
Use the name cards from the chart to transition children from
    group time to the next activity.
Sing other songs that include the names of children (see *More
    Than Singing*, activities 7.7, 7.8, 7.10, 7.11, 7.12, and 7.13).
Clap the syllables of children's names at group time. Later, use
    wood blocks to accentuate the syllables of children's names
    (see *More Than Singing*, activity 3.1).
Place this interactive chart in the music area with several wood
    blocks to encourage children to continue to explore the familiar
    print in a music activity (see *More Than Singing*, activity 5.1).

Helpful Hint

Use a paper punch to
make the holes in the
name cards. Punch
several times to make
the opening large
enough to go over the
paper fastener.

3.2   The Train

Description

This interactive chart continues to build on the children's interest in their names and the names of other children. The chart is in the shape of a train engine. A window in the engine allows each child to insert his or her photo. Children can then add their names to the poem printed on the engine. This interactive chart generates repeated use as children add the photos and names of their friends to the train.

> I looked in the engine
> And what did I see?
> I saw _____
> Looking back at me.

Child's Level

This activity is most appropriate for preschool and kindergarten children.

Materials

- ◆ black poster board, cut in the shape of a train engine
- ◆ gold metallic marker, to write the words of the poem on the train
- ◆ clear acetate or extra lamination film, to form a pocket on the engine for holding the photos
- ◆ name card for each child in the class, printed on heavy paper or sentence strips and laminated
- ◆ self-adhesive magnetic tape, to attach the name cards to the chart

What to Look For

Children will repeat the poem as they add photos and names to the chart.

Some children will point to the words as they read the poem.

Children will compare the way the names look as they change them.

Many children will quickly recognize their own names and the names of other children in the class.

Some children will comment on which names start with the same letter.

Some children will initially just look at the first letter of a name when trying to read it.

Modification

Other cars can be added to the train, with the corresponding poem printed on them and a place for a photo and name. For example, the poem on a boxcar would read, "I looked in the boxcar . . ."

Comments & Questions to Extend Thinking

Can you find the name that matches this picture?

Look at the word "I." It is both a letter and a whole word! Can you find the word "I" again on the chart?

Comments & Questions to Encourage Phonetic Awareness

"See" and "saw" both begin with the same sound.

What word sounds like "see"?

The word engine begins with the letter "e," but I hear the name for the letter "n" when I say the word.

Integrated Curriculum Activities

Read books about trains, such as *Freight Train,* by Donald Crews (New York: Mulberry, 1978); *The Train Ride,* by June Crebbin (Cambridge, MA: Candlewick, 1995); and *Trains,* by Byron Barton (New York: Harper, 1996).

Change the dramatic play area into a train. Just lining up the chairs, one behind the other, often suggests a train to young children.

Sing train songs (see *More Than Singing,* activity 6.12).

Helpful Hint

Laminate the chart after you write the words with metallic marker. Attach the pocket with clear packing tape after the chart has been laminated.

3.3　Snowflakes Are Swirling

Description

This winter poem provides additional opportunities for children to interact with their names and the names of others, observe the letter *s* in several different words, and hear the differences in the sound of the letter in both the initial and final position of a word. This poem encourages children to use their whole body to imitate the movement of snowflakes as they say the poem. The combination of moving the body while saying the words is beneficial to some children as they memorize the poem.

> Snowflakes are swirling
> Softly through the air.
> <u>Everyone</u> likes to catch them
> As they tumble everywhere.

Thanks to Diane Goldman for permission to print this poem.

Child's Level

This chart is most appropriate for preschool and kindergarten children.

Materials

- ◆ dark blue poster board
- ◆ dark blue marker
- ◆ white sentence strips
- ◆ snowflake cutouts, stickers, or illustration, to decorate the chart

- self-adhesive Velcro pieces, to attach the name cards to the chart
- name card for each child and teacher in the class, made from white sentence strip, laminated or covered with clear self-adhesive paper (the name cards should be cut to the exact size of the blank on the chart), and with a small piece of self-adhesive Velcro on the back of each

What to Look For
Children will repeat the poem as they add their names to the chart.
Some children will point to the words as they read the poem.
Many children will recognize their names and the names of others.
Some children will comment on which names start with the same letter.
Some children may notice the repetition of the letter *s* in many words on the chart.

Modification
Add a second interactive element to the chart for older or more experienced children. They can write words for the movement of the snowflakes, such as *blowing, dancing,* or *falling.* This may encourage children to use invented spelling, a picture dictionary, or other resources for spelling these words.

Comments & Questions to Extend Thinking
Can you find the word "snowflake" in the poem?
How many "s's" are in this poem?
How many different places can you find the letter "s" in the poem?

Comments & Questions to Encourage Phonetic Awareness
I can hear the sound for the letter "s" at the beginning of some words and at the end of some words. Can you find a word with the letter "s" at the end of it?
Kevin wants to add his name to the chart. What sound does Kevin start with? What letter should we look for?

Integrated Curriculum Activities
Read snow and winter books such as *Snowballs,* by Lois Ehlert (San Diego: Harcourt, 1995); *The Snowy Day,* by Ezra Jack Keats (NY: Viking, 1962); and *Snow on Snow on Snow,* by Cheryl Chapman (NY: Dial, 1994).
Sing snow songs (see *More Than Singing,* activities 2.6 and 6.6).
Combine white paint and dark blue paper in a painting or printing activity (see *More Than Painting,* chapter 5).

Helpful Hint

Look in craft stores for paper snowflake garlands to use on this chart.

3.4 The Mitten

Claire dropped a mitten
Down in the snow,
In crawled a mouse 🐭
Which made the mitten grow.

Description

This poem is based on the traditional Ukrainian folktale. Each child's name can be added to the chart along with an animal that crawls into the mitten. The names of the children hang on a paper fastener while the animal word cards are attached with a self-adhesive fabric such as Velcro. This prevents children from adding an animal name in place of a child's name.

> <u>Claire</u> dropped a mitten
> Down in the snow,
> In crawled <u>a mouse</u>
> Which made the mitten grow.
>
> ©1997 Sally Moomaw

Child's Level

This chart is appropriate for older preschool, kindergarten, and first-grade children.

Materials

- light blue poster board
- white sentence strips
- black or dark blue marker
- word cards for animals in the book, cut to fit the blank space on the chart
- illustration or sticker of each animal in the book, for the animal word cards
- colored pencils, to color the animal illustration

Helpful Hint

Teachers may download the illustrations of the animals from *The Mitten* illustrator Jan Brett's Web site.

- name card for each child and teacher in the class, made from a white sentence strip and laminated or covered with clear self-adhesive paper (the name cards should be cut to the exact size of the blank on the chart)
- cutouts of a mitten to decorate the chart
- paper fastener, ¾ inch, to attach the name cards to the chart
- self-adhesive Velcro, to attach the animal word cards to the chart

What to Look For

Children will say the poem as they add their name and the animal word cards to the chart.

Some children will point to the words as they say the poem.

Children may compare the letters in the names of the animals to letters in their own names.

Younger children may only be interested in placing their names on the chart.

Some children may attempt to add the animal word cards to match the sequence in the book.

Modifications

Provide pieces of paper with holes punched in them for older children to write the names of other animals to add to the chart.

For kindergarten and first-grade children the animal illustration can be placed on the back of the word card. Children can check the accuracy of their reading of the animal names by looking on the back of the word card.

Comments & Questions to Extend Thinking

Which animal do you want to crawl into the mitten now?

Why do you think the animals made lots of room for the bear?

I notice that the word "mouse" begins with the same letter as "mitten."

Comments & Questions to Encourage Phonetic Awareness

How do you know which word card is "mouse" and which is "mole"? They both begin with the letter "m" and a "mm" sound.

You want to add hippopotamus to the mitten. What sound do you hear at the beginning of the word?

Integrated Curriculum Activities

Compare several versions of the Ukrainian folktale "The Mitten."

Read other books with a similar story structure, such as the traditional folktale *The Turnip,* by Pierr Morgan (New York: Philomel, 1990).

I Went Camping

Description

Children enjoy the predictable book *I Went Walking*, by Sue Williams (San Diego: Harcourt, 1989). This chart uses a similar predictable sentence structure but coordinates well with children's interest in bugs.

> I went camping.
> What did you see?
> I saw <u>an ant</u>,
> Under a tree.

Child's Level

This chart is appropriate for preschool, kindergarten, and first-grade children.

Materials

- ◆ green poster board
- ◆ black marker
- ◆ manila sentence strips
- ◆ word cards for ant, bee, grasshopper, ladybug, beetle, and so on
- ◆ illustrations or stickers of insects, for the word cards
- ◆ illustration of a tent and several insect stickers, to decorate the chart
- ◆ paper fastener, ¾ inch, to attach the insect word cards to the chart

Helpful Hint

Be sure to use *a* or *an* before the insect name on the individual insect word cards rather than on the chart. This allows you to use the appropriate article for each word.

What to Look For

Children will quickly memorize the poem and add an insect word card in the space provided.

Some younger children may believe that the insect names are actually the names of children in the class.

Modification

Ask children to suggest other insects, animals, or camping items that they may see, and make word cards for those suggestions. Provide slips of paper with prepunched holes. Older children can write their ideas for insects, animals, or camping items to add to the chart.

Comments & Questions to Extend Thinking

What insects do you think you might see on a camping trip?

What insects have we seen outside on the playground?

We have a book with pictures of insects. Would you like to make a word card for one of those?

There is a canteen in the dramatic play area for camping. Is there a word card for the canteen?

Comments & Questions to Encourage Phonetic Awareness

I can think of an insect that rhymes with the word "see." Can you guess what it is and how to spell it?

Grasshopper has two "s's" and two "p's," but we can hear only one "s" and one "p."

Integrated Curriculum Activities

Set up the dramatic play area like a campsite, with backpacks, flannel shirts, and a pop-up tent.

Read the book *I Went Walking,* by Sue Williams.

Place a selection of plastic insects and magnifying glasses in the science area with an insect reference book.

3.6 Chicka Chicka Boom Boom

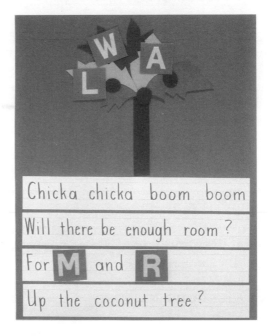

Description

The nonsense words to this traditional chant, incorporated into an interactive chart, introduce children to the alphabet letters. The background of the chart is a giant felt coconut tree. Rubber cement is used to secure the felt to the chart after it is laminated. Children add individual alphabet letters to each of the blanks to complete the poem.

> Chicka chicka boom boom
> Will there be enough room
> For _____ and _____
> Up the coconut tree?

Child's Level

This chart is most appropriate for preschool and kindergarten children.

Materials

- ◆ dark blue poster board
- ◆ white sentence strips
- ◆ black marker

- two shades of green felt for the palm fronds and brown felt for the coconuts and the trunk of the tree
- uppercase alphabet letters mounted on construction paper
- self-adhesive Velcro to attach the alphabet letters to the chart

What to Look For

Some children may initially play with the alphabet letters without reading the chart.

Some children will recite the chant as they place alphabet letters on the coconut tree or in the blank spaces of the chart.

Children may look for the letters of their names.

Some children may attempt to spell their names using the alphabet letters.

Some children will remember the letter names after watching other children use the chart.

Modifications

Include additional vowels so children can spell their names more easily.

The set of lowercase letters can be added, but the quantity of pieces may be overwhelming to many children.

Comments & Questions to Extend Thinking

Which letter will run to the coconut tree first?

Can you find all the letters for your name?

Help me find the letters for my name.

Comments & Questions to Encourage Phonetic Awareness

Look at the "c" and "k" in "chicka." Together they make a "kuh" sound.

What sounds do you hear in "boom"? The two "o's" together make a sound. Listen as I say the word again.

Integrated Curriculum Activities

Include foam alphabet letters in the sensory table with a Plexiglas easel (activity 6.12).

Add alphabet rubber stamps to the writing center (see activity 5.5).

Include alphabet puzzles in the curriculum.

Helpful Hint

Press-on alphabet letters can be mounted on construction paper. This is a quick and easy way to make the movable pieces.

3.7 Bingo Revisited

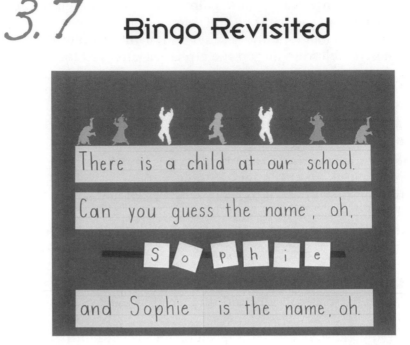

Traditional melody

©1996 Sally Moomaw

There is a child at our school. Can you guess the name, oh,

P E T E R, P E T E R,
EL IZ A B ETH, EL IZ A B ETH,

P E T E R, and Pe-ter is the name, oh.
EL IZ A B ETH, and E-liza-beth is

Description
This chart uses names of the children in the class in place of Bingo in the popular children's song. Children can spell out the names of other children and sing them as they read the chart.

Child's Level
This chart is appropriate for older preschool and kindergarten children.

Materials
◆ red poster board

- white sentence strips
- black marker
- self-adhesive magnetic tape, to attach the alphabet letters and names to the chart
- silhouette stickers, to decorate the chart
- markers in various colors, for printing the children's names on 1-by-2-inch construction paper pieces (use a different marker color for each child's name)
- envelopes, for storing the individual letters for each child's name

What to Look For

Children will sing the song and place the letters of their names on the magnetic tape as they sing.

Some children may begin by using a different child's name that begins with the same first letter.

Some children may be able to sing the song but need assistance placing the letters on the chart.

Children may enjoy separating the individual letters into the appropriate envelope for each child.

Modification

Switch to regular magnetic letters when children are more confident in spelling their names. The magnetic letters will also stick to the magnetic tape.

Comments & Questions to Extend Thinking

Whose name starts with a "k"?

I found the "b." What other letters will I need for "Brianna"?

Which child has the longest name?

Comments & Questions to Encourage Phonetic Awareness

Which name starts with the same sound as "Caitlyn"?

Which letter makes the sound at the end of "Will"?

I hear the sound "ee" at the end of several of names—Mollie, Casey, Andy, and Jamie. Not all of those names end with the letter "e."

Integrated Curriculum Activities

Refer to the tape from *More Than Singing* to hear a recording of this song (activity 2.11).

Read alphabet books such as *Chicka Chicka Boom Boom,* by Bill Martin Jr. and John Archambault (NY: Simon & Schuster, 1989).

Helpful Hint

Print each child's name on the outside of the envelope using the same color marker that was used for the letters of that child's name. This makes it easier to sort the names into the correct envelopes.

3.8   Scarf Dancing

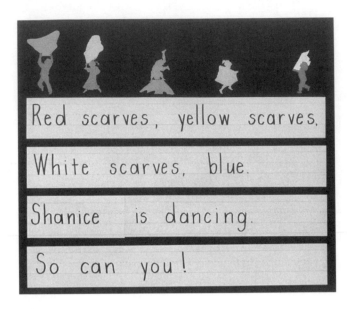

Red scarves, yellow scarves,

White scarves, blue.

Shanice   is dancing.

So can you!

Description

This interactive chart coordinates well with the book *Color Dance,* by Ann Jonas (New York: Greenwillow, 1989). The poem encourages children to move their bodies as they dance with colorful scarves. Children add their names to the chart in place of the word *everyone.*

> Red scarves, yellow scarves,
> White scarves, blue.
> <u>Everyone</u> is dancing.
> So can you!

Thanks to Louise Phillips for permission to reprint this poem.

Child's Level

This chart is appropriate for preschool and kindergarten children.

Materials

- ◆ black poster board
- ◆ white sentence strips
- ◆ black marker
- ◆ silhouette stickers and construction paper cut in the shape of a flowing scarf, as pictured, to decorate the chart
- ◆ name card for each child and teacher in the class, made from white sentence strips, and laminated or covered with clear self-adhesive paper (the name cards should be cut to the exact size of the blank on the chart)
- ◆ ¾-inch paper fastener for attaching the name cards

What to Look For

Children will recite the poem as they add their names.

Some children will dance as they recite the poem.

Some children will point to the words as they recite the poem.

Some children will begin to recognize the color words after interactions with the chart.

Some children may notice the repetition of the word *scarves* in the poem.

Modifications

Provide other color word cards to replace the word *yellow* in the poem.

Add a paper fastener above the word *yellow*. Some children may wish to write their own color words to place on the chart.

Comments & Questions to Extend Thinking

Can you help Stephen find the word "everyone"?

How many times can you find the word "scarves" in this poem?

Help me read the chart with this name on it.

Comments & Questions to Encourage Phonetic Awareness

"Yellow" begins with the letter "y," but your name ends with the letter "y."

I hear the sound for the letter "s" at the beginning and at the end of the word "scarves."

The word "scarves" has an "a" in it, but I can't hear that sound.

Shannon wants to write "green." What sounds do you hear in "green?"

Integrated Curriculum Activities

Set up the dramatic play area as a dance area, with ballet and tap shoes, costumes, and scarves (see *More Than Singing*, activity 6.15).

Include color words at the writing center (see activity 5.4).

Read other books about dancing such as *Lion Dancer*, by Kate Waters and Madeline Sloveny-Low (New York: Scholastic, 1990); *Mimi's Tutu*, by Lynia Thomassie (New York: Scholastic, 1993); and *Silent Lotus*, by Jeanne M. Lee (New York: Tarrar, 1991).

Introduce materials associated with dance, such as ribbon or tulle, into the art area (see *More Than Painting*, activity 2.14).

Helpful Hint

The jacket from the book *Color Dance* can also be used as the illustration to decorate the chart.

3.9   Pizza Is Yummy

> Pizza is yummy
>
> We like it a lot
>
> La'Sean likes tomatoes best
>
> On the top!

Description
Children like to select their favorite pizza topping to include on this interactive chart. They also like to add their names and the names of their friends to the chart.

> Pizza is yummy.
> We like it a lot!
> La'Shawn likes pepperoni best
> On the top!
>
> ©1996 Sally Moomaw

Child's Level
This interactive chart is appropriate for both preschool and kindergarten children.

Helpful Hint

Use very small pieces of Velcro on the backs of the pizza-topping word cards. This makes removing the cards from the chart easier for children.

Materials
- brown poster board
- manila sentence strips for the poem
- brown marker
- illustration of pizza
- name card for each child and teacher in the class, made from white sentence strips, and laminated or covered with clear self-adhesive paper (the name cards should be cut to the exact size of the blank on the chart)

- word cards for pizza toppings such as *cheese, mushroom, pepperoni, tomatoes,* and *green pepper,* cut to the exact size of the blank on the chart
- illustrations of pizza toppings for the word cards
- ¾-inch paper fastener to attach the name cards
- self-adhesive Velcro to attach the pizza-topping word cards

What to Look For

Children will repeat the chant as they add their names and favorite pizza topping to the chart.

Some children may add the topping but not change the name of the child.

Many children will begin to recognize the differences in the spelling of the pizza-topping words.

Children may comment on the spelling of *pepper* in both *pepperoni* and *green pepper.*

Modifications

Place the picture cue for the pizza topping on the back of the word card. Older preschool and kindergarten children can verify their reading of the word by checking the back of the card.

Provide slips of paper for children to write different pizza toppings. They can use cellophane tape to attach the paper to the chart.

Comments & Questions to Extend Thinking

Can you find the word "pepper" on two word cards?

What topping will you add to your pizza?

The word card for "green pepper" has the same letter repeated more than once. Can you find the letters that repeat?

Comments & Questions to Encourage Phonetic Awareness

Nilani is looking for the word "cheese." What should she look for to find that word card?

You want to add "sausage" to your pizza. What sounds do you hear in the word?

Integrated Curriculum Activities

Set up the dramatic play area as a pizza restaurant with aprons, tablecloths, pizza boxes, menus, and order pads (activity 7.9).

Have children vote for their favorite pizza topping.

Make pizzas as a cooking activity.

Clap the syllables for pizza toppings (see *More Than Singing,* activity 3.13).

3.10 Dirty Clothes

Wash your clothes in soapy water.

Hang them up today.

Marker, paint, and milk,

Soon will fade away.

Description
Young children love to wash doll clothes in the sensory table. This interactive chart encourages them to think of all the things they get on their clothes to make them dirty.

> Wash your clothes in soapy water.
> Hang them up today.
> Marker, paint, and <u>apple juice</u>,
> Soon will fade away.
>
> ©1995 Brenda Hieronymus

Child's Level
This chart is appropriate for older preschool and kindergarten children.

Materials
- white poster board
- light blue sentence strips
- black marker
- illustration of clothes drying on a clothesline, to decorate the chart

- clear acetate or extra lamination film, to form a pocket on the chart for holding the word cards made by the children
- slips of paper, cut to fit into the clear pocket, for children to add words

What to Look For
Children will repeat the poem as they add their suggestions to the chart.
Some children may point to the words as they read the poem.
Some children may ask for assistance spelling or writing the words they add to the chart.
Some children may draw pictures of the items to add to the chart.

Modification
For younger children, word cards with picture cues (milk, grape juice, ketchup) can be provided as well as slips of paper for children to create their own words.

Comments & Questions to Extend Thinking
What kinds of things at school can stain your clothes?
Let's look for the word "mustard" in the dictionary.

Comments & Questions to Encourage Phonetic Awareness
Listen to the words "today" and "away." Can you hear the same sound at the end of each word?
You said chocolate milk stains your clothes. "Chocolate" starts with the same letters, "ch," as "cheese." Can you think of other foods that start with the same sound?
Alice wrote "m-k" on her card. She says she spilled "milk" on her shirt.
I got glue on my clothes today. What sound does "glue" start with?

Integrated Curriculum Activities
Set up the dramatic play area as a laundry, with cardboard washer and dryer, as well as a clothesline and clothespins for hanging up clothes.
Allow children to wash doll clothes outside in the sensory table and hang them to dry on a clothesline attached to the fence.

Helpful Hint

Take a photograph of clothes drying on a clothesline to use for the illustration on the chart.

3.11 Hurry Mama

Hurry mama, hurry mama,

Hurry Charles fast.

Hurry bring the pacifier

So that baby's cries won't last.

Description

This interactive chart incorporates key words associated with caring for a baby. As they sing the song children exchange their names for *mama* and select a word card for a baby item to exchange for *bottle*.

©1996 Sally Moomaw

Hur - ry Ma - ma, hur - ry Ma - ma, hur - ry Ma - ma fast.

Hur - ry, bring the bot - tle so that ba - by's cries won't last.

Hurry Mama, hurry Mama
Hurry <u>Mama</u>, fast.
Hurry, bring the <u>bottle</u>
So that baby's cries won't last.

Child's Level

This interactive chart is appropriate for both preschool and kindergarten children.

Helpful Hint

Baby catalogs are a good resource for pictures of baby items.

Materials

◆ blue or other pastel poster board
◆ white sentence strips
◆ black marker
◆ name card for each child and teacher in the class, made from white sentence strip, and laminated or covered with clear self-adhesive paper (the name cards should be cut to the exact size of the blanks on the chart)
◆ word cards for *bottle, rattle, blanket, diaper, pacifier,* and so on, cut to the exact size of the blank on the chart
◆ stickers or illustrations of baby items, for the word cards
◆ illustrations of crying babies, to decorate the chart
◆ ¾-inch paper fastener, to attach the name cards
◆ self-adhesive Velcro, to attach the baby item word cards

What to Look For

Children will add their names and the names of their friends to the chart.
Many children will recognize the word *mama* on the chart.
Some children may want to add other family members, such as daddy or grandma, to the chart.

Modification

Include a pocket made of clear acetate at the end of the third line for older children. They can write the word for the item they want to bring for the baby.

Comments & Questions to Extend Thinking

Look: The first three lines all start with the same word.
Can you find the word "mama" somewhere else on the chart?

Comments & Questions to Encourage Phonetic Awareness

What sound does "bottle" start with? Do you know what letter makes that sound?
What word sounds like "fast"?
Listen to the word "mama." The same sounds repeat: "ma-ma."

Integrated Curriculum Activities

Set up the Baby Writing Center (activity 5.12).
Set up the dramatic play area as a baby nursery with extra babies, bottles, blankets, rattles, and clothes.
Wash babies in the sensory table.
Make a class book based on the song "Hurry Mama" (activity 2.4).
Make family greeting cards with the children (activity 4.13).

Writing Explorations

Nilani pretended to bake a cake in the dramatic play area. She shook an empty cake box over a bowl, stirred the bowl with a wooden spoon, and placed the bowl in the oven. Then she decided she wanted to keep the recipe. With paper and pencil from a nearby writing box, Nilani carefully began to copy the ingredients from the back of the cake box. A short while later, she showed her writing to the teacher. "Look," Nilani said. "This is how you make a cake."

▲ ▲ ▲

Sijia was busy typing on the classroom computer, which was part of the writing center. She took class name cards, one at a time, from a basket and typed the words on the computer. Sijia carefully watched as the letters appeared in large type on the screen. Each time she completed a name, Sijia pressed the enter key. Soon she had a list of all the names in the class. Sijia's teacher then helped her print the list on the printer.

▲ ▲ ▲

Children are excited about writing, especially when it serves a purpose, such as advancing their play or preserving important information. Teachers can capitalize on this natural interest in writing by designing specific materials to incorporate into play activities or planning activities to highlight the writing process.

Teachers' Questions

How does writing emerge in young children?

Writing emerges in young children in predictable stages. During the initial **scribbling** stage, children make global approximations of writing. Next, in the **linear/repetitive** drawing stage, they refine their scribbles to appear more like personal cursive. Writing at this level often looks like scallops or waves. This stage is followed by closer approximations of letters in the **letterlike forms** stage.

Next, during the stage of **letters and early word–symbol relationships,** children actually print letters but may use a single letter to represent an entire word. Phonetic awareness becomes apparent in the following stage, **invented spelling,** as children begin to write the sounds they hear. Finally, children progress to the stage of **standard spelling.**[1] See chapter 1 for a more complete description of the stages, and examples.

At what age do children become interested in writing?

Children often become interested in writing early in their preschool years, once they develop sufficient coordination to control a writing implement. This does not mean that they immediately begin to produce recognizable print. Writing emerges gradually as children experiment with writing materials and become more aware of written language.

How do young children usually hold the pencil?

Children often progress through a series of pencil grasps as they progress in their ability to write. Initially, many young children wrap all four fingers around the pencil in a **fist grip.** Some children wrap all four fingers around the pencil but also rotate the hand so that the back of the hand faces the body in an **overhand grip.** Later many children develop a **three-finger grip,** with two fingers on top of the pencil and the thumb opposite. A **tripod** grip, the most mature grasp, is the standard writing position characterized by one finger on top of the pencil, one finger below the pencil, and the thumb opposite. Many older preschool children hold the pencil with a tripod grasp; however, some children continue to hold the pencil near the eraser end for a while, which often contributes to faint, wobbly handwriting. Three-finger grips, or even fist grips, are still used by some kindergarten children, particularly if they have not had much experience with writing.

Should the teacher correct a child's pencil grasp?

The teacher should not correct a child's pencil grasp, because it is not a mistake to hold the pencil in a less mature grasp. Rather, it shows the child's current level of development. Children usually hold the pencil in the manner that is most comfortable for them. Gradually, as they develop more hand and finger strength and better coordination, they change grips. When teachers insist that children hold the pencil in a particular way, they may inhibit and discourage children from trying to write. If a teacher senses that a child is becoming frustrated with writing due to a particular way of holding the pencil, then the teacher may choose to model an alternative grip. This should be offered as a suggestion rather than an ultimatum.

What concepts do children construct through early writing experiences?

Early writing experiences help children construct concepts related to the meaning of print and the mechanics of written communication. Before children can use print as a symbol system to communicate their thoughts, they must understand that print has a specific meaning. Writing activities such as story dictations (activity 4.3), creating class books (activity 4.12), and pocket stories (activity 4.1) help children construct this fundamental concept. Children also learn specific mechanics of writing, such as left-to-right and top-to-bottom text progression and the need for a particular sequence of letters in order to form specific words. In addition, children gradually learn the function of capital letters and certain punctuation marks.

How can teachers encourage the emergence of writing in young children?

Teachers can facilitate children's transition into writing by accepting all writing attempts as legitimate, helping children see the component parts of letters or words, and incorporating writing into daily routines. As children begin to try to express themselves through writing, it is crucial that adults acknowledge their attempts as communicative, just as they respond to babies' babbling as a real form of communication. This encourages children to continue experimenting with the writing process. The teacher might acknowledge an early writing attempt by saying, "I see a lot of writing underneath your picture." If the teacher cannot decipher the child's writing, he might say, "Tell me what you were thinking about when you wrote this." Understanding the normal stages of writing helps teachers and parents appreciate the written forms that children demonstrate.

Teachers can help children who are developmentally ready progress to more advanced stages of writing by isolating parts of letters or words. However, it is crucial to accurately judge the child's developmental readiness. Children need many opportunities to experiment with writing materials before they acquire the coordination to produce particular strokes. Trying to rush them through the process may cause unnecessary frustration and discourage children from writing. Many children advance through the writing stages without any outside assistance; however, some children seem to benefit from the teacher scaffolding their learning by breaking down the letters or words as they move from one stage to the next. For example, if a child has become proficient at producing linear, repetitive drawing, isolating the circular and straight parts of a letter may be a catalyst for helping them produce more letterlike forms. For children who are in the letterlike form stage, describing or modeling how a particular letter is formed may help them create closer approximations. Teacher intervention should be to encourage rather than evaluate, with the goal always to support the writing process rather than dampen enthusiasm. Therefore, teachers may choose to offer assistance primarily when they notice that a child is becoming frustrated.

Many daily occurrences provide reasons for children to write if teachers incorporate them as classroom expectations. For example, many teachers use waiting lists to help children wait for turns at popular activities. Rather than writing the children's names for them, teachers can give that responsibility to the children. This creates a real motivation to write. Of course, teachers must accept writing at any stage as legitimate and not critique children's attempts, or they may quickly become discouraged. Other natural situations that may motivate children to write are putting names on artwork, writing messages about seat placement at lunch, and creating save signs for block structures. Children can be given responsibility for all of these tasks. Baskets of name cards strategically placed around the classroom may help children who need a model for writing their names. Incorporating writing throughout the classroom is also discussed in chapter 7.

What materials do young children need for writing activities?

Children need a variety of types of writing tools and both lined and unlined paper. On the one hand, younger children often feel more comfortable writing with a marker than a pencil since they may not yet have enough finger strength to create a dark mark with a pencil. On the other hand, children see adults writing with pencils, so they are eager to try them. The more experience children have with pencils and other writing devices, the stronger their fingers become. Adults often assume that "fat" pencils are easier for children to hold. Actually, when given a choice, children often prefer regular-width pencils to the wider ones.

Children who are just transitioning into writing may be inhibited by lined paper. Since children's first attempts at creating letterlike forms are usually large and shaky and placed randomly on the page, it is unrealistic for children to try to fit them between the lines. Later, when children begin to refine their writing and gain better control, lined paper provides a useful guide for their writing.

What types of writing activities are developmentally appropriate?

Dictation, extensions of predictable text, story starters, and documentation of specific activities or projects encourage children to experiment with writing. Children must first construct concepts about written language before they can begin to write. Story dictation helps them perceive the relationship between written and spoken language and can serve as a bridge to actual writing (activity 4.3).

Just as predictable text supports the emergence of reading, it can also stimulate children's writing. Creating greeting cards based on a repeating text (activity 4.13) or altering the words to popular songs (activity 4.4) are examples of writing activities based on a predictable format.

Story starters are a useful tool in motivating children to write. An image of a favorite story character (activity 4.2) or an open-ended phrase (activity 4.13) are two types of story starters teachers can use as writing catalysts.

Documentation of activities or group projects provides a natural forum for writing. Since children often tell stories as they create with art materials, teachers can capitalize on the natural link between art and language by combining art and writing activities (activities 4.9 and 4.14). Long-range group projects require documentation in order to preserve the thinking process that propels the project. Children can help with the documentation (activities 4.7 and 4.20). They may also be interested in recording their experiences on field trips (activity 4.11).

What should teachers consider when taking dictation?

Teachers should write exactly what children say, regardless of possible grammatical errors, and create clear print models. While it is tempting to correct any language mistakes children may make, this causes confusion when they attempt to read what has been written. As they look at the corrected words, they mentally repeat what they originally said but see something different on the paper. Children gradually correct their grammatical errors as their language develops. While teachers will certainly want to model correct grammar when they talk to children, the goal for dictation is not to set spoken language models but to help children construct an accurate relationship between spoken and written language.

Seeing their words written down encourages children to begin writing themselves.

Teachers should print clearly when they take dictation from children. Since young children are just beginning to learn how written language looks, they cannot distinguish letters written in various styles. Therefore, the teacher's printing should be in a standard form that closely resembles the print children see when they look at books. Teachers should write in lowercase letters, use correct capitalization and punctuation, and allow an adequate space between words so that children can distinguish where one word stops and another word starts.

What should teachers do if a child avoids writing?

Teachers should continue to provide encouragement and include opportunities for writing in areas of the classroom where the child feels comfortable. Sometimes children avoid writing because they feel that their writing is not good enough. They may have been teased by an older sibling or criticized by an adult. As children observe teachers accepting and encouraging writing on all levels, they may feel confident enough to try writing themselves. When writing materials are available throughout the classroom, children may incorporate them into their play and feel less threatened about perceived writing inadequacies. Teachers often observe that some children produce far more writing in the dramatic play area than in the writing center.

How can teachers incorporate writing throughout the curriculum?

Teachers can include writing materials as functional parts of area designs throughout the classroom. For example, if the dramatic play area is transformed into a dance studio, writing tickets could be a logical outgrowth of the play in that area. An observation notebook might be included in the science area, since careful observation is part of the scientific process. Children may wish to write words to fit on a song chart in the music area, while in the art area they may record stories or descriptions for their artwork. One group of children designed an amusement park in the block area of their classroom, complete with signs labeling the various rides. If teachers can envision possible writing activities as they design areas of the classroom, then children are more likely to incorporate writing into their play.

How can teachers incorporate journal writing into early childhood classrooms?

Teachers may include journal writing as a regular part of the class schedule or make journal writing available whenever children are interested. Journal writing is scheduled as a regular part of the day in many kindergartens and first-grade classrooms. While children may be encouraged to write about whatever they wish, they may all write at a particular time of the day. This allows the teacher to assist a number of children during journal time and ensures that all children spend some time writing each day.

Preschool teachers may prefer to make journals available as a choice activity rather than as a structured part of the day. Each child in the class can have a journal folder that they add to whenever they are interested. Teachers can encourage journal writing by providing paper in unusual shapes, word cards that are of interest to the children to use as models, and a variety of writing implements. (See activity 4.15 for journal ideas.) With children's permission, teachers may choose to read children's journal entries to the class during group time.

How can teachers encourage phonetic awareness through writing activities?

Teachers can help children hear the sounds of words they are attempting to write and draw their attention to sound–letter relationships. Children are interested in phonics when it is an outgrowth of the writing process. Teachers can help children distinguish various sounds by emphasizing them as they repeat a particular word that a child is writing. Since initial consonants are the first sounds that children learn to distinguish, emphasizing the beginning sounds of words is a good starting point. Later, teachers can focus on ending sounds, interior consonants, and vowel sounds. Teachers should scaffold for children who are using phonetic spelling. For example, if the child can already distinguish the initial sound, then the teacher can ask what other sounds the child hears, and emphasize them.

How can teachers assess children's development of writing skills?

Teachers can record anecdotal notes that describe each child's writing progress and save examples throughout the year. Some teachers maintain a folder for each child that includes anecdotal records and also samples of the child's work. Other teachers keep a notebook with pocket dividers to section off a space for each child. Teachers should be careful to record details about the child's writing, including which hand was used, how the child held the writing implement, what stage of writing appeared, how long the child engaged in writing, and where in the classroom the activity took place. Such detailed notes help teachers monitor children's writing progress and also plan additional activities that build on the interest of the children. Writing strategies and outcomes can be quickly recorded on the writing assessment form in appendix D.

How can teachers explain emergent writing to parents?

Teachers can include information about writing stages in newsletters and discuss the writing process during open houses or parent meetings. Parents can support children's emergent writing when they understand the normal progression of children's development in writing. Seeing specific examples of the various stages is especially helpful. Parents come to view their children's writing attempts as important steps in a long-term process and become excited when they see new stages emerge.

How can teachers use writing activities to bridge home and school?

Teachers can design writing activities and materials to send home and display project documentation for parents to see. A classroom prop such as a small teddy bear can rotate among homes and serve as a writing catalyst. Parents can help their children document what they did with the bear, and children can share the written account when they return to school with the bear (activity 4.16). A literacy suitcase, which contains a variety of writing materials, can also circulate among homes. Literacy suitcases are discussed in chapter 8.

Parents are naturally interested in class projects and events. Documentation boards, which may also include samples of children's writing, keep parents informed about important learning experiences at school.

1. Marjorie V. Fields, "Talking and Writing: Explaining the Whole Language Approach to Parents." *The Reading Teacher,* vol. 41, no. 9 (May 1988): 898-903.

Writing Activities

pumpkin

4.1   Pocket Stories

Description
Pocket stories allow children to see their words in print and also to match the words. For this activity, the bottom of a piece of paper is folded up about two inches and stapled to form a pocket. Each child draws a picture and then dictates a phrase or sentence about the drawing, which the teacher prints on the pocket. The teacher then prints duplicate words on strips of paper, which the child can match to the words in the sentence and store inside the pocket. Children can also copy the words or add their own writing to the pocket.

Child's Level
This activity is appropriate for preschool, kindergarten, and some first-grade children.

Materials
- manila paper, 9 by 12 inches, with the bottom edge folded up and stapled to form a pocket
- strips of paper, to print duplicate words that can be cut apart and matched to the words on the pocket
- markers

What to Look For
Children will eagerly match the individual words to the words in the sentence on their pocket.

Some children will copy the individual words or the entire sentence.

Some children will create their own pocket stories with art or writing materials.

Helpful Hint

Fold up at least two inches for the pocket, or the word cards will fall out easily.

Children will look at each other's pocket stories.

Some children will notice punctuation and word placement.

Modification

Teachers of older or more experienced children may wish to write the original sentence on the pocket themselves in order to create a clear model, but have the children print the duplicate words to go into the pocket.

Comments & Questions to Extend Thinking

Tell me about your picture. I'll write your words on this pocket.

Can you find the word on your pocket that matches this word?

Look at the word "I." It's a letter and a word.

Comments & Questions to Encourage Phonetic Awareness

Listen to the sound this word starts with. What letter do you think I need to write?

What sounds do you hear in this word?

Can you find another word in your sentence that starts with the same sound as this word? (Clearly pronounce the initial consonant.)

Integrated Curriculum Activities

Put paper folded into pockets in the art or writing areas. Children may wish to continue creating pocket stories.

Share the pocket stories at group time. Children are often interested in hearing what their friends have written.

Create a group pocket story. Children can collaborate on a group mural and dictate a short story about it. The teacher can fold up a pocket at the bottom and create word cards for matching.

4.2 Story Starters

Example dictated by the child

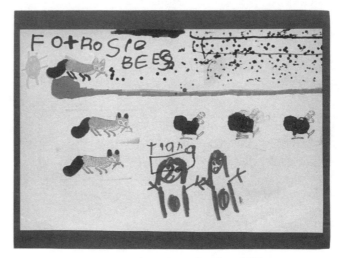

Example written by the child

Description

This activity encourages children to draw and write about a familiar character from a book. Children start by creating a rubber stamp impression of the character on their paper. They then complete the picture however they choose. Children can write or dictate their own stories to go with their pictures.

Child's Level

This activity is appropriate for older preschool, kindergarten, and first-grade children.

Materials

◆ story paper (blank at the top and lined at the bottom), 12 by 18 inches, or manila paper, 9 by 12 inches
◆ rubber stamp of a familiar book character
◆ markers

What to Look For

Children who are just learning the relationship between spoken and written language will eagerly examine the written words as they repeat what they dictated.

Some children will write their own stories. They may use phonetic or standard spelling, depending on their stage of development.

Some children will use nonstandard placement patterns for the words.

Some children will dictate what they want to say, but then add some of their own writing, perhaps in personal cursive.

Some children will copy what the teacher writes.

Modification

Encourage older children to do their own writing by supplying word cards with the names of the characters. Accept phonetic spelling.

Comments & Questions to Extend Thinking

What is "Corduroy" doing in your picture?

Here is a word card for "Strega Nona" if you need to see how her name is spelled.

Tom used the word "ran" in his story too. Ask him to show you how he spelled it.

Comments & Questions to Encourage Phonetic Awareness

Lynn wants to write "mouse" in her story. What sound does "mouse" start with?

This is interesting. "Kitty" and "cat" both start with the same sound, but a different letter represents the sound.

You need the letters "s" and "h" together to make that sound.

Integrated Curriculum Activities

Have copies of the books that go with the character stamps available in the reading area.

Put story paper in the art or writing areas so children can continue to illustrate and write stories.

Helpful Hints

Children's bookstores often have rubber stamps that match book characters.

Some book characters, such as the fish from *Swimmy,* by Leo Lionni, can be cut from a sponge.

4.3 Pumpkin Books

Description
Children must construct concepts about written language before they can begin to write. Shape books that have blank pages inside often motivate children to dictate stories. They can then compare the written words to what they said. Children may also decide to add writing of their own or create pictures to go inside the book.

Child's Level
This activity is most appropriate for preschool and kindergarten children.

Materials
- orange construction paper, cut into a pumpkin shape, for the front and back covers of each book
- inexpensive white paper, also cut into a pumpkin shape, for the interior pages, with four pages allotted per book
- markers
- word cards, made from index cards or sentence strips, with relevant words such as *pumpkin* or *jack-o-lantern* clearly printed on them

What to Look For
Some children will dictate stories. They will compare the spoken words to the printed words.
Some children will add their own writing to the books.
Children will write at various levels depending on their stage of development.

Helpful Hint

Pumpkin-shaped notepads can also be used for the covers of the books.

Modification

Encourage older children to do their own writing by supplying
word cards with key words. Accept phonetic spelling.

Comments & Questions to Extend Thinking

What would you like to say in your pumpkin book?

Here is how the word "pumpkin" looks. You can copy it if you
want to when you need it in your story.

I see lots of "p's" in this book. I think Andy is writing about
pumpkins.

Comments & Questions to Encourage Phonetic Awareness

Listen to the word "pumpkin." What sounds do you hear?

Does "jack-o-lantern" start with the same sound as "pumpkin"?

Integrated Curriculum Activities

Take a field trip to a pumpkin patch before writing the pumpkin
stories (activity 4.11).

Put a variety of pumpkins in the science area. Let children guess
what is inside before opening one (see *More Than Magnets*,
activity 2.6).

Estimate how many grooves are on a pumpkin and record
the children's responses (see *Much More Than Counting*,
activity 3.4).

4.4 Helping Baby

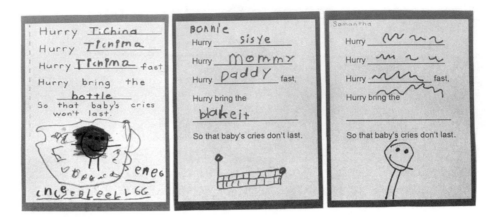

Description

A familiar song (see activity 3.11 for the music) can serve as the basis for an exciting writing experience. In this activity, children write new words for a baby song, including what baby needs and who should bring it. The repetitive text helps children transition into reading since they can readily see words that look alike.

> Hurry _____, hurry _____,
> Hurry _____, fast,
> Hurry, bring the _____
> So that baby's cries don't last.
>
> ©1996 Sally Moomaw

Child's Level

This activity is most appropriate for older preschool or kindergarten children.

Materials

- photocopy paper, in assorted colors, with the words to the song printed on each page and blank spaces for the item baby needs and the person who will bring it (see illustration)
- blank photocopy paper, for children who wish to write all the words to the song
- markers

What to Look For

Many children will write their own names in the appropriate spaces in the song.

Some children will use phonetic spellings for the baby items they want to add to the song.

Some children will write using personal cursive, letters, or letter-like forms.

Children will attempt to read the words to the song.

Some children will remember the spellings for certain words from the song, such as *baby*.

Modification

Older or more experienced children may wish to write all of the words to the song rather than just filling in the blanks.

Comments & Questions to Extend Thinking

What baby item do you want to write on your page?

This word says "hurry." Can you find that word any other place on your page?

I'll write "Grandpa" for you on the first line, and then you can write it on the next two lines.

Comments & Questions to Encourage Phonetic Awareness

What sounds do you hear in the word "bottle"? What letters do you need to write for those sounds?

What word in the song sounds like "fast"?

I see "t-b" on this page. Alice says her baby is getting a teddy bear.

Do you hear any other sounds in the word "drum"?

Integrated Curriculum Activities

Read a big-book version of "Hush, Little Baby" to the class (activity 2.6).

Create a class baby book using baby pictures of each child (activity 2.4).

Estimate how many baby pacifiers will fit in a clear jar (see *Much More Than Counting*, activity 3.1).

Helpful Hint

The pages can be stapled together or bound with a spiral binder to form a class book.

4.5   Bought Me a Cat

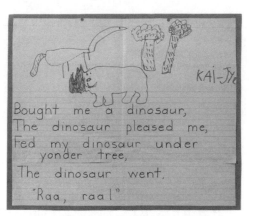

Example dictated by the child

Example written by the child

Description

Children love silly songs and delight in the traditional folk song "Bought Me a Cat." Once children are familiar with the words, they can introduce animals of their choice into the song along with the sounds they make. Some children may dictate their song versions while others can write the words themselves.

Traditional

Child's Level

This activity is most appropriate for older preschool or kindergarten children.

Materials

- story paper (blank on the top half and lined on the bottom half), 12 by 18 inches
- markers

What to Look For

Children will enjoy selecting animals to add to the song.

Some children will dictate their words for the song.

Some children will use phonetic spelling for the sounds the animals make.

Some children will write using personal cursive, letters, or letter-like forms.

Children will attempt to read the words to the song.

Some children will know the standard spelling for certain animals.

Modification

If the song requires too much writing for early writers, preprint all of the words to the song except for the animal name and the sound it makes.

Comments & Questions to Extend Thinking

What animal do you want to add to the song?

I wonder if the word "tiger" is in the class dictionary. What letter should we look under?

Comments & Questions to Encourage Phonetic Awareness

Alice says her animal growls. What sounds do you hear in the word "growl"?

What word in the song rhymes with "me"? Look: "Tree" ends with two "e's," but "me" only has one "e."

I'm thinking of an animal that starts with a "duh" sound. What do you think it could be?

Helpful Hint

Mount the story paper on construction paper for durability.

Integrated Curriculum Activities

Sing the children's versions of the song at group time.

Read predictable books about animals such as *Dear Zoo*, by Rod Campbell (Washington, DC: Four Winds, 1982).

Transform the dramatic play area into a veterinary office, with stuffed animals, stethoscopes, and white shirts for lab jackets.

Create a big-book version of the familiar song "Old MacDonald" (activity 2.10).

4.6 Surprise Box

Description
Children love to make guesses about surprises. In this activity, a classroom surprise is wrapped in a box. The children take turns guessing what's in the box and write their guesses on the wrapping.

Child's Level
This activity is most appropriate for preschool or kindergarten children.

Materials
- surprise box, with a solid color of wrapping paper
- dark marker

What to Look For
Children will be excited about guessing what's in the box.

Children will write at various levels, depending on their stage of development.

Some children may wish to cover the entire box with writing. Teachers may decide that each child can write one idea on the box and the rest on paper.

Modification
Younger children may prefer to have the teacher write their guesses on the box so they can see what the words look like.

Helpful Hints

Wrap the package with as many layers of paper as there are children in the class. When it is time to open the box, each child can have a turn removing a layer of wrapping.

If possible, use a permanent marker to write the guesses on the box. Otherwise, the print may smear.

Comments & Questions to Extend Thinking

What do you think is in the box? Do you want to write your idea
on the box?

Tell me what you were thinking about when you wrote your guess.

John wants to know what your guess was, Tina. Can you read it
to him?

Comments & Questions to Encourage Phonetic Awareness

Look. Nori guessed "candy" and Hinako
guessed "cat." They both start with the same
sound and letter.

Mark thinks there's a box inside the box. What's
the last sound in the word "box"?

Integrated Curriculum Activities

Read books about surprises, such as *When This Box Is Full*, by
Patricia Lillie (New York: Greenwillow, 1993) and *Happy Birth-
day, Sam*, by Pat Hutchins (New York: Viking, 1978).

Create a surprise-box musical instrument. Each side of the lidless
wooden box is a different height. Children can listen for how
the size of the wood affects the sound (see *More Than Magnets*,
activity 6.9).

4.7 Science Observations

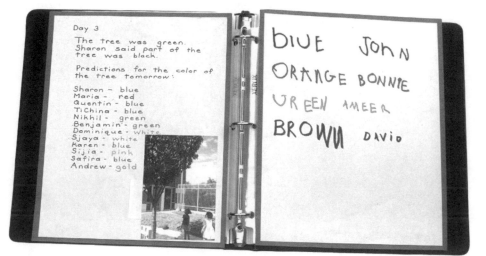

Description
This activity links science and literacy. Many science activities encourage children to make predictions and detailed observations. In this activity, children carefully observe a tree in autumn. Each day they predict what color the tree will be on the following day. They record their observations in a notebook, which also includes daily photographs of the tree.

Child's Level
This activity is appropriate for preschool, kindergarten, and first-grade children.

Materials
- loose-leaf notebook
- pencils or markers
- word cards, to provide a written model of frequently used words
- daily photographs of the tree

What to Look For
Some children will be very interested in observing the tree and recording their predictions.

Some children will not be interested in the project until the tree begins to change colors.

Many children will have unusual predictions for the color of the tree due to their limited experience and their stage of cognitive development.

Children will write at various levels, depending on their stage of development.

Children will reread previous predictions each day.

Modification
Younger or less experienced children may prefer to have the teacher write their predictions in the notebook so they can see what the words look like.

Comments & Questions to Extend Thinking
What color is the tree today? What color do you think it will be tomorrow?

What color did Amy write in the notebook?

You can use these word cards to help you write your prediction.

Comments & Questions to Encourage Phonetic Awareness
Are there any colors that start with the same sound?

Can you tell what the vowel sound is in the word "red"? (This question is for older children.)

Listen to the long "e" sound in "green." Look: It has two "e's" together.

Integrated Curriculum Activities
Children may wish to broaden the observation of trees by participating in a long-term project such as growing a tree or creating a tree for the classroom.

Take a field trip to look at more trees. A walk through a park or a visit to a nursery are possibilities.

Create leaf rubbings by placing lightweight paper over leaves and rubbing over the leaves with crayons.

Sing songs about trees in autumn (see *More Than Singing*, activity 2.5).

Helpful Hint

Cover the pages with clear page protectors to preserve the writing samples and the photos.

4.8 Word Processing

Description

The computer can be a useful tool for encouraging emergent writing. In this activity, a computer is set to a large print size so children can easily view the results of their typing. The font is Arial, or a similar style, which is close to the standard print that children use. Teacher-constructed boxes cover the function and control keys to prevent children from inadvertently opening other applications.

Child's Level

This activity is appropriate for older preschool, kindergarten, and first-grade children.

Materials

- ◆ classroom computer with word-processing software
- ◆ poster board and plastic tape, to construct small boxes to cover the function and control keys
- ◆ print samples, such as class names or relevant words from a thematic topic, project, or book

What to Look For

Children will experiment by pressing keys and observing what comes up on the screen.

Many children will begin to type specific words.

Children will learn to use the space bar, the shift key, and the enter key.

Helpful Hint

Since you will need the mouse to open and close the program, keep it behind the computer while the children are typing. This limits problems caused when they click on the tool bar.

Many children will wish to produce a hard copy on a printer if one is available.

Children will learn to match upper- and lowercase letters since the letters on the keyboard are capitals, but the letters that appear on the screen are lowercase.

Modification

Older children, or children who have had more experience with computers, may not need to have the function and control keys covered.

Comments & Questions to Extend Thinking

Can you find the letter on the computer that looks like this?

The letters on the keyboard are capital letters, and the letters on this word card are lowercase. Type the letter "A" on the computer and see what comes up on the screen.

Press the "enter" key and see what happens.

Comments & Questions to Encourage Phonetic Awareness

Sarah made a list of names on the computer. Do any of these names start with the same sound?

What sounds do you hear in "tiger" (or whatever word the child wishes to type)? Can you find the letters for those sounds on the computer?

Integrated Curriculum Activities

Put the children's word banks (see activity 6.1) by the computer. Children may wish to type the words on the computer.

Use the computer to create class books. Each child can add a page to the book.

4.9 Quilt Stories

Description
For this activity, children first draw a picture and then write or dictate a description or story about it. The stories are framed individually with pieces of wallpaper. They are then mounted together to produce a giant class story quilt. Children can read their friends' stories or have an adult, parent, or older child help them.

Child's Level
This activity is appropriate for preschool, kindergarten, or first-grade children. Although many preschool children do not yet draw representationally, they often like to name their drawings and talk about them.

Materials
- story paper (blank on the top and lined on the bottom), cut in half vertically
- wallpaper scraps cut to form a border around each story
- assorted markers for drawing and writing

What to Look For
Children will be interested in seeing how their spoken words look on paper.
Some children will want to write at least part of their story.
Children who are doing their own writing will write at various levels, depending on their stage of development.

Helpful Hint
Laminate the framed stories if possible. This will make them much more durable.

Modification

Some children may prefer to write on unlined paper. They can use regular paper for their drawing and a separate sheet of paper to write on. The two papers can then be stapled together.

Comments & Questions to Extend Thinking

This is what Mengyi said I should write. "I make a cat." (Point to each word as you read.)

Brady wants to write the word "zebra." Do you think "zebra" is in our class dictionary?

Carina put lots of writing on her paper. This must be a long story!

Comments & Questions to Encourage Phonetic Awareness

How does "fire truck" start? (Emphasize the "f" sound.) You can write that sound first. What sound do you hear next? (Focus on the word the child is trying to spell or the word the child has asked for help with.)

You wrote "ct" for cat. I hear those sounds too.

Look: "Dog" starts with a "d" sound and so does "Doug."

Integrated Curriculum Activities

Create other types of quilts with the class. Children can sew with large needles on pieces of burlap (see *More Than Painting*, activity 6.5).

Read books from various cultures that focus on the meaning behind quilts. Examples include *Sweet Clara and the Keeping Quilt*, by Deborah Hopkinson (New York: Knopf, 1993); *Luka's Quilt*, by Georgia Guback (New York: Greenwillow, 1994); and *The Keeping Quilt*, by Patricia Polacco (New York: Simon & Schuster, 1988).

4.10 Class Post Office

Description
Mailboxes and envelopes seem to encourage children to write. For this activity, the dramatic play area is transformed into a post office with a mailbox for each child. Props include paper, envelopes, stamps from advertisements, and purses that look like mail bags.

Child's Level
This activity is most appropriate for preschool and kindergarten children.

Materials
- individual mailboxes, made from hollow wooden blocks, gallon or half-gallon milk cartons, or a divided shelf
- writing materials, such as paper, envelopes, markers, pencils, and stamps from advertisements
- purses, to use as mail bags
- blue shirts or jackets, to resemble mail-carrier clothes

What to Look For
Children at all stages of writing will write messages to put in their friends' boxes.
Many children will look at the names on the mailboxes and attempt to copy them onto their envelopes.

Helpful Hint

Teachers can encourage emergent reading by putting messages in the children's mailboxes.

Some children will take on the role of mail carrier. They will look closely at the names on the boxes as they attempt to deliver the mail to the right person.

Modification
First-grade children may want to set up a mail system with other classes.

Comments & Questions to Extend Thinking
This message is for Brian. Can you help me find his box?
Can you help Mark read the message you wrote to him?
You can use this basket of name cards to help you write your friends' names.

Comments & Questions to Encourage Phonetic Awareness
I'm going to write "hi" on my note. Help me listen for the sounds.
What letter do you think "love" starts with? Listen while I say the word. (Emphasize the starting sound of the word the child is trying to write.)
My message says "luv." I'm going to say each sound and see if I can read the word. "L—u—v." I think my message says "Love, Nina."

Integrated Curriculum Activities
Read books about mail such as *A Letter to Amy,* by Ezra Jack Keats (New York: Harper Collins, 1968) and *Mail Myself to You,* by Woody Guthrie (Glenville, IL: Good Year Books, 1994).
Create math games with a mail theme (see *More Than Counting,* activities 4.10, 5.6, and 5.16).
Let the children draw pictures or write notes to mail home. Walk to a mailbox in small groups to mail them.
Assemble a literacy suitcase based on a mail theme (activity 8.5).
Create a class "mail book" (activity 2.5).

 **Pumpkin Patch**

Field Trip Documentation

Description

Field trips are exciting experiences for children; therefore, they are usually eager to help document them. For this activity, each child is photographed during a trip to a pumpkin farm. Later the children write or dictate captions for the photographs, which are then mounted on documentation boards or assembled into a class book.

Child's Level

This activity is appropriate for preschool, kindergarten, or first-grade children.

Materials

- ◆ photograph of each child, taken during the field trip
- ◆ paper and markers, for writing captions to go with the photos
- ◆ poster board, 22 by 28 inches, for mounting the photos and written documentation

What to Look For

Children will eagerly recount their memories of the trip when they see the photos.

Some children will dictate their ideas.

Helpful Hint

Order duplicate prints of the photographs. One photo can be used on a documentation panel and the other put into a year-end scrapbook for each child.

Children who wish to write their observations will write at various levels, depending on their stage of development.

Children will be eager to share their stories with one another.

Children who cannot yet read will carefully attend to the print as an adult reads about each child.

Modification

Younger or less experienced children may prefer to dictate their remembrances to the teacher so they can see what the words look like when written down. Older children can be encouraged to do their own writing.

Comments & Questions to Extend Thinking

Tell me about this picture.

What did you do with the pumpkin after you picked it? (This encourages the child to elaborate and think sequentially.)

What did your pumpkin feel like when you picked it up?

Comments & Questions to Encourage Phonetic Awareness

What sound do you hear at the beginning of "pumpkin"? What letter do you think makes that sound?

What other sounds do you hear in "pumpkin"?

I hear an "n" at the end of "pumpkin." Listen. (Emphasize the "n" sound at the end of the word.)

Integrated Curriculum Activities

Read books about pumpkins, such as *Pumpkin Pumpkin,* by Jeanne Titherington (New York: Greenwillow, 1986).

Document classroom activities, such as cooking, in the same way.

Use small novelty pumpkins as counters for a math game.

Make pumpkin-shaped blank books for the children to write in (activity 4.3).

4.12 All About Us
Class Book

I'm as playful as a puppy.

I'm as little as a ladybug.

I'm as big as a dinosaur.

Quentin
I'm as funny as a crab. I am like Batman. I think about a moon. I will make a spaceship.

Nikhil
I'm as playful as a puppy. I'm as happy as a lark. I'm as brave as a tiger.

Description
Children return again and again to books they create as a class. In this group book, the children each describe themselves. Since the writing project is introduced after the children have become very familiar with Audrey Wood's predictable book, *I'm As Quick As a Cricket,* the children often incorporate the simile sentence construction "I'm as . . ." into their descriptions of themselves.

Child's Level
This activity is appropriate for older preschool, kindergarten, or first-grade children.

Helpful Hint

Mount the stories on construction paper and laminate before combining them into a book. This greatly increases their durability.

Materials
- story paper (blank on the top and lined on the bottom)
- sentence starters, with the simile construction, to use as models
- markers

What to Look For
Children will enjoy creating fanciful descriptions of themselves and seeing how their ideas look in print.

Some children will notice words that repeat, such as *as.*

Children who do their own writing will write at various levels, depending on their stage of development.

Children will enjoy reading each others' descriptions or listening to an adult read them.

Modification

Younger or less experienced children may prefer to dictate their descriptions to the teacher so they can see what the words look like when written down. Older children can be encouraged to do their own writing. Sentence starters, such as those pictured, may help.

Comments & Questions to Extend Thinking

How would you describe yourself? "I'm as . . ." (Pause while the child thinks.)

Fumi says he's as strong as an elephant. Can you find where it says "elephant" on his page?

Comments & Questions to Encourage Phonetic Awareness

Who has an idea for how to write the "fuh" sound in "elephant?"

"F" is a good suggestion for that sound, but this time "p" and "h" together make the "fuh" sound.

Ann wants to write "big." What sound does "big" start with?

Integrated Curriculum Activities

Include *I'm As Quick As a Cricket*, by Audrey Wood (Singapore: Child's Play Ltd., 1982), in the reading area.

Read a big-book version of *I'm As Quick As a Cricket*. (See chapter 2 for ideas about making big books.)

Create self-portraits. Children can look in cosmetic mirrors and then draw themselves.

4.13 "Family Day" Cards

Description

For this activity, children elaborate on a recurring phrase from a predictable book as they create cards for their families. Since not every child has a mother and a father, any family member or caregiver can be the recipient of the card. The recurring phrase is "I love my _____ because . . ." This activity is introduced after the children have become familiar with the books *I Love My Mommy Because . . .* and *I Love My Daddy Because . . .*, both by Laurel Porter-Gaylord (New York: Dutton, 1991).

Child's Level

This activity is appropriate for preschool, kindergarten, and first-grade children.

Materials

- ◆ colored photocopy paper, folded in halves or fourths to create cards
- ◆ markers

What to Look For

Children will be eager to write their sentiments on the cards.

Some children will wish to create many cards for various family members.

Children will write at various levels, depending on their stage of development.

Helpful Hint

The opening statement on the cards can be preprinted on a computer if desired. Use a font that looks like standard print, such as Arial.

Modification

For younger or less experienced children, preprint the recurring phrase. They can write or dictate the individualized portions. Older or more experienced children can write the whole sentiment.

Comments & Questions to Extend Thinking

Who will get this card?

Can you find a card that says "mommy"?

This card says, "I love my grandma because . . ." What do you want to add to the card?

Comments & Questions to Encourage Phonetic Awareness

I hear lots of "m" sounds in "mommy." Look at all the "m's."

What sounds do you hear in "daddy"?

A "y" can sound like "ee" at the end of a word. Look at the end of "mommy" and "daddy."

Integrated Curriculum Activities

Read other books about families such as *The Mommy Book* and *The Daddy Book*, both by Ann Morris (Parsippany, NJ: Silver Press, 1996).

Put multicultural toy families in the block area. Children can create their own dollhouses with the blocks.

4.14 Cloud Stories

Description

For young children, art and writing are often closely related. For this activity, children create straw-blown paintings with white paint on dark blue paper. They then alter the words to a cloud song to describe their paintings.

Words by Peter Moomaw   ©1980 by Sally Moomaw

I saw some clouds a-blow-ing way up in the sky.

I thought I saw so ma-ny things as the clouds went drifting by.

> I thought I saw a _____
> Way up in the sky,
> I thought I saw a _____
> As the clouds went drifting by.

Child's Level
This activity is appropriate for older preschool, kindergarten, or first-grade children.

Materials
- dark blue construction paper, 9 by 12 inches
- white tempera paint, thinned with water
- straw for each child, to blow a dab of paint across the paper
- white photocopy paper, for writing the words to the song

What to Look For
Children will create imaginative words to accompany their
   paintings.
Children will be able to "read along" since they already know the
   words to the song.
Some children will prefer to dictate their words so they can see
   how they look in print. They may then add writing of their own.
Children who produce their own writing will write at various
   levels depending on their stage of development.

Modification
For younger or less-experienced children, preprint the recurring
   phrase. They can write or dictate the words that describe their
   pictures. Older or more experienced children can write all the
   words.

Comments & Questions to Extend Thinking
What does your painting remind you of? You can write that on
   the song sheet.
I see lots of letters on your paper. Tell me what you were writing
   about.

Comments & Questions to Encourage Phonetic Awareness
Candace wrote "hs" on her paper. I'm going to say those sounds.
   Listen! Candace saw a "horse."
David saw a dragon. What letter does he need to write first?

Integrated Curriculum Activities
Sing the cloud song on the playground on a sunny day. Children
   can look for shapes in the clouds and add them to the song.
Create other kinds of cloud pictures. Cotton balls, white crepe
   paper, white fabric, white wallpaper, and Styrofoam pieces
   could be used.
Sing the children's versions of the song at group time.

Helpful Hint
Prick a hole in each straw with a pin. Children can still blow paint through the straw but will not be able to suck it in.

Description

Journal writing is incorporated into many kindergarten and first-grade classrooms. At first, most children seem to enjoy it; however, over time some children get tired of journal writing. Since teachers want to cultivate an enjoyment of writing in children, this activity gives ideas for inspiring young writers by connecting journal writing to other areas of the curriculum. Paper cut into specific shapes, and word cards tied to areas of high interest, encourage renewed interest in journal writing.

Child's Level

This activity is most appropriate for kindergarten and first-grade children.

Materials

Shape of paper

- *grocery cart*, to encourage children to write shopping lists, perhaps to use in dramatic play or for a field trip
- *ice cream cone*, to coordinate with an ice cream parlor in dramatic play
- *space ship*, to build on children's interest in space
- *mitten*, to tie into children's interest in the book *The Mitten*, by Jan Brett
- *heart*, to coordinate with interest in Valentine's Day

Word cards

- favorite foods generated by the children, such as pizza, chocolate milk, ice cream, and pretzels
- ice cream flavors, such as vanilla, chocolate, strawberry, and mint
- rocket, astronaut, robot, blast-off, moon, stars, comet, sun, and galaxy
- animals from the story, such as rabbit, fox, hedgehog, bear, and owl
- candy-heart phrases, such as "Be Mine," "Hug Me," and "I Love You"

What to Look For

Some children will find it easier to decide what to write because the paper and words give suggestions.

Many children will be eager to write on the unusual paper.

Children will write at various levels depending on their stage of development.

Children will be interested in what their friends write on the fancy paper.

Modification

For preschool children, teachers can incorporate journal writing as a choice activity for interested children.

Comments & Questions to Extend Thinking

What would you like to write on the heart-shaped paper?

Here are some words that you might want to use in your space story.

Who has an idea for an interesting shape of paper to use next week?

Comments & Questions to Encourage Phonetic Awareness

This word card for "moon" has two "o's" together. Listen to the sound they make.

Write the sounds you hear in the words you want to write. We can look up spellings later.

Integrated Curriculum Activities

Read some of the journal entries at group time. Check with the children to be sure they want to share their journals.

Cut paper into interesting shapes to add to the writing center.

Helpful Hint

Shapes as small as stickers can easily be enlarged on a photocopy machine to create a pattern for the paper.

4.16 Take-Home Bear

Description
This activity links home and school. Children take turns bringing home a small teddy bear. As part of the experience, they write or dictate a story about what they did with the bear. They may write at home with their parent or at school after they return with the bear. The stories are compiled into a journal that all of the children can look at.

Child's Level
This activity is appropriate for preschool, kindergarten, and first-grade children.

Helpful Hint

Send a note home with the bear so parents know when to return it.

Materials
- small teddy bear
- gift bag or small backpack, for transporting the bear
- loose-leaf notebook, for compiling stories about the bear

What to Look For
Children will be eager to share their stories about "Take-Home Bear."

Children will discover that each story sounds the same each time it is read.

Children who do their own writing will write at various levels, depending on their stage of development.

Older children may demonstrate a mixture of phonetic and standard spelling.

Modification

Younger or less experienced children may prefer to dictate their stories so they can see how the words look. They may add some of their own writing later. Older children may do the bulk of the writing themselves.

Comments & Questions to Extend Thinking

What do you want to say about "Take-Home Bear"?

Do you want to read your story about Take-Home Bear to us, or should we look at it together?

Comments & Questions to Encourage Phonetic Awareness

I'm going to read all the sounds Kim wrote. "Tk hm br." It says "Take Home Bear"!

Look at the word "take." The "e" on the end changes the sound of the "a."

What sounds do you hear in "bear"?

Integrated Curriculum Activities

Read books about teddy bears, such as *When the Teddy Bears Came,* by Martin Waddell (Cambridge, MA: Candlewick Press, 1994).

Put paper shaped like a teddy bear in the writing area. Children may wish to use the paper to write more stories about teddy bears.

Create teddy bear math games (see *More Than Counting,* activities 4.7, 5.3, and 5.14).

4.17 Address Books

Description
As the end of the year approaches, many children are interested in keeping in touch with one another. They are thus highly motivated to create class address books. This activity introduces children to the standard form used to write addresses.

Child's Level
This activity is appropriate for older preschool, kindergarten, or first-grade children.

Materials
- construction paper, 9 by 12 inches, folded in half to create the front and back of each book
- white photocopy paper, 8½ by 11 inches, also folded in half, for the interior pages
- cards with the names and addresses of the children in the class, to serve as models

What to Look For
Many children will copy at least some of the names and addresses. At first, some children will not understand the necessary placement of the words to form an address.

Helpful Hint

Be sure to have parent permission before releasing addresses.

Younger children may ask the teacher to copy the information. They may then add writing of their own to the book, perhaps in personal cursive or letterlike forms.

Modification
Younger children may be overwhelmed by the amount of writing involved. Teachers can make the task less daunting by having the children write the names and an adult write the addresses.

Comments & Questions to Extend Thinking
Whose name is on this card?
Peter is looking for your address card. Can you help him find it?
This is the street you live on, and this is the city.
"St." is an abbreviation. It means "street."

Comments & Questions to Encourage Phonetic Awareness
I'm looking for Doug's address. What letter does his name start with?
We can abbreviate "North" by just writing the first letter. What sound do you hear at the beginning of "North?"
Amanda wants to abbreviate "West." What do you think the first letter is?

Integrated Curriculum Activities
Read the book *Mail Myself to You,* by Woody Guthrie (Glenville, IL: Good Year Books, 1994) to the class.
Put a post office in the dramatic play area (activity 4.10).
Create a stamp collection for sorting and classifying. (See *More Than Counting,* chapter 3, for information about collections.)

4.18 Writing Caddies

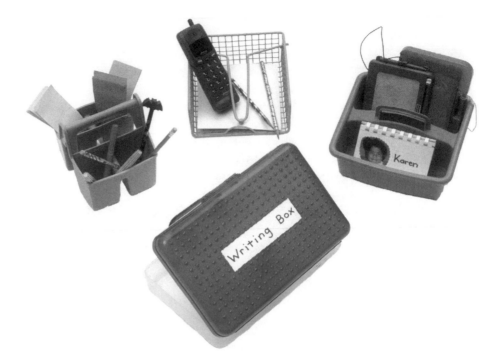

Description
Since children often incorporate writing into their play, having writing materials strategically placed throughout the classroom encourages emergent writing. This activity shows several ways that writing materials can be organized in various areas of the classroom.

Child's Level
This activity is appropriate for preschool, kindergarten, and first-grade children.

Helpful Hint

Save samples of the children's writing from around the classroom. They can be included in a portfolio assessment.

Materials
◆ silverware caddy with paper strips, pencils, and markers, placed in the block area
◆ small Magna Doodle drawing toy, or a writing slate, included in a basket with a booklet of class names, in the manipulative area
◆ small basket with paper and pencils, located near the pretend telephone in the dramatic play area
◆ small plastic carrying case containing paper and markers, for children to carry to various areas of the classroom where they wish to write
◆ small spiral notebook and pencil, located in the science area, for children to record their observations

What to Look For

Children will write throughout the classroom with materials in the writing caddies.

Some children who do not typically use the writing center will write with materials from the writing caddies.

Modification

Teachers can vary the placement of the writing materials depending on classroom organization or design. For example, some first-grade classrooms do not have a dramatic play area but may need more observation notebooks in the science area.

Comments & Questions to Extend Thinking

If you want to sit by Joseph at lunch, get the writing caddy and write a message so I don't forget.

Be careful. That block building has a sign on it. You can ask Tiffany what she wrote.

I can't come to the phone now. Will you take a message?

Comments & Questions to Encourage Phonetic Awareness

Luis wants to write a stop sign for the cars in the block area. What sounds do you hear in "Stop"?

Sanjay thinks the coconut has water inside. He wants to write his prediction in the notebook. What letter do you think "water" starts with?

Integrated Curriculum Activities

Create additional writing caddies to take outside. Children may use them for a variety of purposes, including keeping score for various games.

Literacy suitcases can also be sent home to encourage writing (see chapter 8).

4.19 Scrapbooks

Description

School scrapbooks, which document each child's development throughout the year, are an excellent way to encourage children to write, preserve each stage of the writing process, and share milestones with parents. The scrapbooks include photographs, writing samples, artwork, and school artifacts, such as name tags and favorite class recipes. Specific pages allow children to record school memories, such as their friends, their favorite lunch, special books, familiar songs, and favorite activities.

Child's Level

This activity is appropriate for preschool, kindergarten, and first-grade children.

Materials

- one inexpensive loose-leaf notebook per child
- photographs of each child engaged in school activities
- page protectors, to hold artwork and writing samples
- multiple photocopies of paper with preprinted headings such as "My Friends," "My Favorite Lunch," "My Favorite Books," "Field Trips," "Class Projects," and "My Favorite Songs"

What to Look For

Children will be eager to help compile their scrapbooks.
Children will read and reread their scrapbooks.
Parents will especially appreciate the documentation of their children's year at school.

Modification

Younger preschool children may need to dictate their lists of favorites to the teacher in order to preserve them. Older preschool and kindergarten children can often assist with the writing, while first graders may be able to do all of the writing themselves.

Comments & Questions to Extend Thinking

Do you want to use the basket of name cards to help you write the names of your friends?
These are some of the books we read this year. Which ones were your favorites?
What were you doing in this picture? Let's write that down.

Comments & Questions to Encourage Phonetic Awareness

Two of your friends have names that start with the same sound. What letter do they start with?
Philip says pizza was his favorite lunch. What letters will he need to write in order to spell "pizza"?

Integrated Curriculum Activities

The scrapbook integrates all of the year's activities.

Helpful Hint

Assemble the scrapbooks throughout the school year. They will be virtually completed by the end of the year.

4.20 Class Movie

Description

In this activity, various types of documentation are used as children create their own class movie. Group projects support emergent literacy through the collaborative efforts of children and teachers. As children explore group projects, appropriate documentation helps them remember their experiences and plan further explorations. Teachers may start the documentation process by recording children's dialogues as they discuss and work on a project. They may make documentation boards to display these dialogues with photographs of the work in progress. This supports emergent reading. Older or more-experienced children may write some of the documentation themselves.

This project starts with each child choosing what character he or she would like to be in the movie. Then a group of interested children writes a story to incorporate all of the characters. The teacher facilitates by asking leading questions such as, "What is happening at the beginning of the movie?" "What will _____ do in the movie?" "Then what happens?" Next, the children decide what costumes and set designs they will need, and they create those. Finally, the teacher narrates and videotapes the movie as the children act out their roles.

Helpful Hint

Teachers should plan to do the videotaping themselves. This enables them to stop the camera whenever necessary.

The Power Rangers, Cat, Rainbow Colors Movie

by Sally's Class

One day, three cats were playing ball in the castle. They said "meow" to each other.
The Princesses were in the castle dressing up. One of the Kings was in the castle putting on his King clothes, and another King was busy sewing King clothes.
Two Queens were chopping down trees to get firewood. They needed the firewood to cook dinner. They took the firewood back to the castle so they could cook dinner. They made chicken noodle soup.
The two Kings, the two Princesses, and the Prince all came running to eat their dinner of chicken noodle soup. But the flames of the fire got too high, and they started to burn the castle!
The two Princesses yelled, "Everyone out of the castle," and the two Kings called 911 to get the firefighters to come and put out the fire. They all escaped from the castle.

The firefighters came in their fire helicopter. They squirted water from their hoses onto the flames and put the fire out.
One cat jumped out of the window to get away from the fire. Two Power Rangers came and helped one cat get out of the castle, and the firefighters helped the other cat get out of the castle.
The Princesses, the Queens, and one cat went to the lake to take a bath. Suddenly, a monster and an alligator jumped into the water and tried to eat the Princesses and the cat, and they were afraid.
The Prince came, and he grabbed the alligator and threw it into the water. The two Power Rangers grabbed the monster and threw it into the water. The Queen came and fought with the monster. The alligator chased after the Kings, and they ran away.
The two Power Rangers made a robot alligator. The tied the robot alligator and the alligator to the castle to guard the castle. The put the monster on top of the castle so he couldn't get off and scare people any more.
Then they all went into the castle. The Prince turned a movie on, and they all watched the movie. They ate popcorn and chips with the movie.

Child's Level
This activity is appropriate for older preschool, kindergarten, and first-grade children.

Materials
- ◆ poster board, for mounting photos and written documentation
- ◆ chart paper, for listing the characters in the movie and the names of the children
- ◆ paper and markers, for children to use as they write and draw ideas for the movie
- ◆ video recorder, for taping the movie
- ◆ materials to create costumes, props, and set designs, as determined during the course of the project

What to Look For
While all children will be involved in the project, children will participate in varying degrees on particular phases of the project. Children will collaborate to create the story for the movie. Many children will pay close attention to the written cast list.

Modification
Older children can be encouraged to do some of the project documentation themselves, such as writing lists of characters and ideas for the story.

(continues on p. 128)

Script by a child

Comments & Questions to Extend Thinking

Who has an idea for a name for the movie? I'll write down all of the ideas, and then we'll vote.

How can I tell from this chart who's playing the part of Batman?

Comments & Questions to Encourage Phonetic Awareness

Will wants to be a king in the movie. What sound does "King" start with?

Listen to the beginning of "queen." "Q" and "u" go together to make that sound.

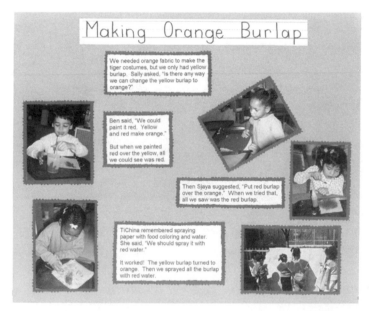

Project documentation

Integrated Curriculum Activities

Invite the parents to a showing of the movie. Attendance will be high!

Help children dramatize familiar stories such as *King Bidgood's in the Bathtub,* by Audrey Wood (San Diego: Harcourt Brace, 1985).

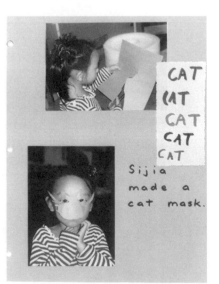

Child's documentation

CHAPTER 5

Writing Centers

Keisha, whose parents had recently separated, cried each day when her mother was ready to leave the center. Although the teacher was able to comfort Keisha, the transition into the center often required the mother to stay for twenty to thirty extra minutes. The mother was becoming more concerned about Keisha's behavior, her own conflicting feelings, and the number of times she was late to work. After two weeks, the parent and teacher decided to minimize the transition time, even if Keisha was still unhappy when her mother left. The teacher sat with Keisha and suggested that they could write a note to Keisha's mother. Keisha agreed, and they went to the writing center to begin. Keisha dictated a message as her teacher wrote, "Mommy don't leave me. I want you to stay at school." Keisha appeared to feel more comfortable after this and allowed her mother to leave. This routine continued for several more days and periodically for the next month, but Keisha was more willing and more able to comfortably separate from her mother each morning.

▲ ▲ ▲

Will and Andy, both almost five, wanted to sit together at lunch. The teacher suggested that they write a message to remind her of the request. Both boys immediately went to the writing center but weren't sure how to begin. The teacher told each boy to write his name on the same piece of paper. She told them she would help them write the word lunch. *Each boy could write his name from memory. The teacher asked if either of them could figure out how to spell* lunch. *They both said the word out loud several times. Will was very excited as he recognized the connection between the sound at the end of his name and the sound at the beginning of the word* lunch. *The teacher spelled the rest of the word and suggested that each boy add the word* lunch *to his word bank so they could always write that message.*

Children often see adults in their environment engaging in meaningful writing activities. Parents write messages as they talk on the phone, make grocery lists, and jot down directions. Teachers create waiting lists for classroom activities and write down children's dictations for a class book. Children begin to recognize the power of print and are eager to participate in this communication system. Early childhood classrooms should include a specific activity center to capitalize on the children's high interest in the printed word.

Teachers' Questions

What is a writing center?

A writing center is an area of the classroom designed to encourage children to experiment with both handwriting and creative writing. Although this center is a permanent part of the classroom design, the materials and activities change periodically to stimulate explorations, reflect the interests of the children, coordinate with other curricular materials, and incorporate both long-term and short-term literacy goals.

Why is the writing center an important part of early childhood classrooms?

Writing centers provide children with materials for explorations in writing as well as opportunities to watch others experiment with writing. Writing centers give children meaningful reasons to copy print, compare letters and words, and express their thoughts, ideas, and feelings. As children transition into writing, they need an environment that encourages them to express themselves, affords easy access to paper and writing implements, and provides a convenient space for experimenting with writing. A writing center provides ample opportunities for children to spontaneously explore writing, for teachers to acknowledge all writing attempts, and for parents to observe the value of a developmentally appropriate approach to writing.

How should a writing center be set up?

Writing materials should be neatly displayed on a table so that children have ready access to the supplies. The table should be large enough to comfortably accommodate two or three children at one time so they can socialize and share information as they write. Whenever possible, the center should be located against a wall, the back of a shelf, or a pegboard divider. This provides space for the display of children's writing samples, environmental print (labels, signs, and other printed materials found in the classroom environment; see chapter 7), and illustrations to enhance the aesthetic appeal of the center or to coordinate with a specific topic. The writing supplies should be attractively displayed so they are inviting to children. Desk and drawer organizers, which are inexpensive and durable, allow children to find the supplies they need and keep the writing surface uncluttered. Children are less motivated to use an area if the materials become jumbled and damaged.

What materials should be included in a writing center?

The writing center should include a selection of paper, writing implements, an alphabet sample, and cards with the names of the children and teachers in the class. These materials are typically displayed throughout the year. Teachers may vary the colors of paper and the design of the pencils to ensure continued interest in the area and to coordinate with other curricular activities. For example, the teacher might select pastel paper, primary colors of paper, or shades of blue at different times throughout the year. Suggestions for how to display the materials and select paper and pencils are included in each activity.

What additional materials can teachers include in the writing center?

Teachers may include blank books, fill-in-the-blank papers, word cards, and a movable alphabet, such as alphabet rubber stamps and plastic or foam letters. Teachers may coordinate these materials with high-interest books, dramatic-play themes, or seasonal changes. The teacher should consider the interests, experiences, and developmental levels of the children when selecting additional materials. These materials often stimulate renewed interest in the writing center, provide additional reasons for children to explore writing, and build on their previous experiences. For example, the teacher might add blank books to encourage children to copy meaningful print or write messages and stories, or fill-in-the-blank papers to encourage children to copy their names, the names of other children, or word cards. Teachers might occasionally include materials such as dry-erase boards, slates, and small Magna Doodle–brand magnetic drawing boards as part of the design of the writing center. These items may be less threatening to some children since the images they write can be erased quickly. Suggestions for selecting materials are found in the individual activities in this chapter.

What are the pitfalls of selecting additional materials for the writing center?

The display of too many materials at one time, which does not leave sufficient space for children to use the materials, may inhibit interest in writing or cause conflicts between children. Children require enough space to write without bumping into other children sitting at the table. When the table is cluttered, children may not be able to locate the specific paper, word card, or pencil they need.

Paper that is too small, cut into specific shapes, or highly decorated may encourage some children to color instead of write. Fancy paper and small pieces of paper may not provide sufficient space for the larger writing produced by younger children. They may choose to color paper shaped like an ice cream cone or fill in the hearts on a piece of notepaper. Older children, however, may be motivated to use notepaper to write a letter, imitating what they have seen adult writers do with fancy paper.

How often should the materials at the writing center be changed?

The length of time the materials remain in the writing center depends on the interests of the children. Two to three weeks is typical, with slight changes or additions as needed. A change in the colors of the paper, the decoration on the pencils, and even the arrangement of the materials stimulates renewed interest in familiar supplies. Teachers often coordinate the word cards in the writing center with high-interest curricular activities. For example, the teacher might include word cards for the characters in the book *Silly Sally,* by Audrey Wood. Children are often interested in reading the names or copying the print.

What kinds of paper and writing implements are appropriate for use at the writing center?

Inexpensive photocopy paper, which is available in a wide array of colors, is both attractive and easy for children to manipulate as they experiment with writing materials. Teachers should explore free sources of computer paper and office paper, from local businesses or parents. Since children associate adult writing with notepads, scrap paper, and other small sheets of paper, teachers may wish to cut paper into smaller pieces. Regular 8½-by-11-inch paper can be cut in halves or in quarters to create different sizes of paper for display. Kindergarten children may be especially interested in more conventional lined paper. Teachers might also want to include other odd sizes of paper or paper cut into interesting shapes.

Conventional office-type pencils are the most appropriate style for young children to use at the writing center. At one time, educators assumed that children needed thick beginner pencils, since the small muscles in the hand are not well developed during the preschool and kindergarten years. Our observations of children indicate that they prefer regular pencils, however.

What are blank books?

Blank books are small paper books made by folding a cover and one or two sheets of white paper together and stapling along the crease. The cover of the book can be made from photocopy paper cut in half, which is both economical and attractive. While construction paper can also be used, it is more expensive. The inside paper should be slightly smaller in length and width than the cover. Teachers can use inexpensive or recycled white paper for the inside of the blank books. Fold the cover and the inside paper together to form the crease. Staple twice along the crease so that the prongs of the staples are on the inside of the book when it is closed. This makes the book lie flat when opened. An office-style stapler will extend a maximum of four inches, so take this into account in planning the book's dimensions. Teachers can use rubber stamps, stickers, or magazine illustrations to decorate the covers of blank books. The decoration can be applied to the original before making multiple copies of the cover.

What are fill-in-the-blank papers?

Fill-in-the-blank papers are typically a predictable sentence from a song, poem, or book printed on a strip of paper, with a blank space for the child to complete by copying from a name card or word card in the space. The teacher creates a fill-in-the-blank sentence to encourage children to copy meaningful print and to understand that changing just one word changes the meaning of the sentence. For example, the teacher might add fill-in papers printed with the sentence "Look who's here, it's _____," which some children recognize as the predictable portion of a popular song from group-time experiences. Children can copy their own names or the names of other children in the blank space. Examples of other suggestions for fill-in-the-blank strips are found in the activities in this chapter.

How are fill-in-the-blank papers different from workbooks?

Teacher-designed fill-in-the-blank papers capitalize on the children's interests of children and have more than one possible word to complete the sentence. Workbooks, on the other hand, are designed to teach a particular concept and typically permit only one correct answer to complete the sentence. The subject of the workbook page may not relate to the interests of the child.

What is a movable alphabet?

A movable alphabet is a set of manipulative alphabet letters such as magnetic, plastic, felt, or wood letters and alphabet rubber-stamp sets. The movable alphabet lets children explore the formation of letters, words, sentences, or entire stories without using a pencil or other writing implement. This is an important tool for children who have not yet developed the ability to form the letters themselves. These children can represent name and word cards with magnetic letters, use the rubber stamps to complete a fill-in-the-blank strip, and write messages that are otherwise too long for their handwriting ability.

What should teachers consider when selecting materials for the writing center?

Teachers should consider the developmental levels of the children, their individual needs, the interests of the group, literacy goals, and opportunities for children to make connections with other curricular materials. The writing center materials are appropriate for preschool and kindergarten children. Younger, less-experienced children may need a simple arrangement of paper, pencils, and name cards, while older, more-experienced children benefit from more extensive writing supplies and opportunities to express themselves. Sometimes the teacher may include a writing activity designed for an individual child that is equally appealing to all children. For example, the teacher may display the alphabet rubber stamps for a child who has difficulty making letters but has high interest in seeing his name in print. The novel materials are appealing to all children and allow the specific child to participate successfully in writing activities.

Should art materials be included at the writing center?

Art materials, such as glue, scissors, and tape, should not be included at the writing center. They take up valuable space at the writing table and may encourage children to damage the writing supplies accidentally. For example, name cards may be taped together or cut in half as children explore the materials in the same ways they do those in an art center.

Teachers may occasionally want to include markers at the writing center. Markers, especially thin markers, closely resemble pencils and may encourage children to explore writing. Several writing center activities at the end of this chapter include thin markers as one of the accessories. For example, colorful markers might stimulate interest in a writing center based on children's interest in the changing colors of the leaves in autumn (activity 5.3) or in the book *Mouse Paint,* by Ellen Stohl Walsh (activity 5.4).

How do children use the materials at the writing center?

Children use the materials in a variety of ways based on their age, experience, and interest. Some children focus more on writing and some focus more on reading. Many children, even very young children, are familiar with paper and pencils and immediately begin to make marks or produce some form of personal print on the paper at the center. Experienced children and children with a high interest in writing may copy name and word cards, write messages, and write on the fill-in-the-blank papers or in blank books. Children advance through a series of predictable stages in the development of writing. Information about these stages and examples of children's writing can be found in chapter 1.

Initially, some children are more interested in reading the name and word cards than in producing marks on paper. Some children are very interested in the name cards and like to read through the set of class names, either independently or with a teacher. Since the connections between reading and writing are so important in the literacy curriculum, teachers should take advantage of opportunities to assist children in creating relation-ships between reading and writing. For example, children often express a desire to save a block structure. Teachers can direct children to the writing center and tailor the writing activity to the individual child's abilities and interests. While a younger child might read her name card and place it on the structure, another child might copy his name to place on the block structure to save it. At a later date, the same child can be encouraged to write his name and additional information, such as "save," on a sign. An older or more experienced child may show interest in writing all or part of a more complex message. Skilled teachers help children understand the connection between reading, writing, listening, and speaking. They take cues from children and scaffold, or build a bridge, between what the children know and what they want or need to do to be successful in communicating through writing.

How can teachers encourage phonetic awareness at the writing center?

Teachers can take advantage of children's natural curiosity about the sounds of the language and relate them to specific reading and writing materials in the writing center. Everyday classroom situations provide a myriad of opportunities for teachers to help children create sound–symbol, or phonetic, relationships. Sometimes the opportunity occurs as children explore the materials at the writing center. For example, if children are interested in reading and writing color words (activities 5.3 and 5.4), the teacher might draw attention to the sound of the *e* in *red* and compare it to the sound two *e's* together make in *green*. When children want to write each other's names, the teacher might help them listen for the initial sound of a name and relate it to the letter or group of letters that create the sound. In this way, children begin to construct phonetic relationships within a context that is relevant and meaningful to them.

Young children, especially older preschool and kindergarten children, delight in creating rhyming words and playing around with the sounds of their language. Teachers can capitalize on this interest by creating a writing center based on a book with strong rhyme, such as *A-Hunting We Will Go* (activity 5.14).

How can teachers set up a computer to allow children to use the word processing?

Teachers can set the computer to a large print size and a font that is as close to standard print as possible, such as Arial or Helvetica. Teacher-constructed boxes, made from poster board, can be taped to the computer to cover the function and control keys. This prevents children from inadvertently opening other applications. Activity 4.8 describes the computer used as a word processor.

Does the inclusion of a computer inhibit children from exploring handwriting?

In many instances, the inclusion of a computer set to function as a word processor encourages handwriting. As children wait for a turn to type, they often explore the other writing materials in the area. When the computer is set up to play games, however, children typically cluster around and watch rather than write.

How can teachers assess children's developmental progress in writing?

Many teachers save samples or make photocopies of children's writing to include in a portfolio, folder, or scrapbook for each child. These samples document children's progress through the writing stages as well as their interest in writing. Teachers can also record anecdotal notes to document details about the child's writing, including how the child grips the pencil, which hand the child uses, and how much teacher assistance was needed or requested.

This information helps teachers monitor children's writing progress, plan additional activities for the group or individual children, and build on the interest of children. Teachers can also use the writing assessment form included in appendix D.

Writing Center
Activities

5.1 Basic Writing Center
Starting the Year

Description
This standard writing center is designed to introduce children to basic supplies for writing activities. The center is well organized and provides children with easy access to paper and pencils. Materials are visually appealing and are contained in attractive boxes and cups. Standard supplies for writing are included along with a name card for each child and teacher in the class.

Child's Level
This basic writing center is appropriate for young preschool children or inexperienced preschool and kindergarten children at the beginning of the school year.

Materials
◆ fancy pencils, one for each place at the writing center
◆ several colors of duplicating paper, cut in half- and quarter-sheets
◆ tomato-paste can, attractively covered with self-adhesive paper, to hold the pencils
◆ name card for each child and teacher in the class, made from an 8-inch section of sentence strip in any color, and laminated or covered with clear self-adhesive paper
◆ containers to hold the paper and name cards

Helpful Hint
Do not use pencils with heavy decorations attached to the top. They may be too difficult for inexperienced children to handle.

What to Look For

Children will experiment with the materials.

Some children may focus attention on the name cards without regard for the writing supplies.

Some children will attempt to copy their names.

Children may display different stages of writing, from random scribble to conventional letter formation.

Some children may not know how to hold the pencil.

A few children may initially write on the table. They can be directed to use the paper.

Modifications

One or more alphabet samples can be added to the center after the children have had an opportunity to explore the basic supplies.

Include small slates or Magna Doodle–brand magnetic drawing boards.

Comments & Questions to Extend Thinking

What can you write with the pencil?

Let's look for your name in the name card basket.

Would you like to read the names of all the children in your class?

Comments & Questions to Encourage Phonetic Awareness

Your name starts just like my name, with "Br" for "Brenda" and "Brianna."

There are two children named Molly in this class, but one Molly ends with "y" and one Mollie ends with "ie."

Integrated Curriculum Activities

Include the names of children on an attendance chart and song chart, such as "Look Who's Here" (activity 3.1).

Clap the syllables in children's names as a way to introduce them to each other at group time and focus on their names (see *More Than Singing*, activity 3.1).

Apple Writing Center

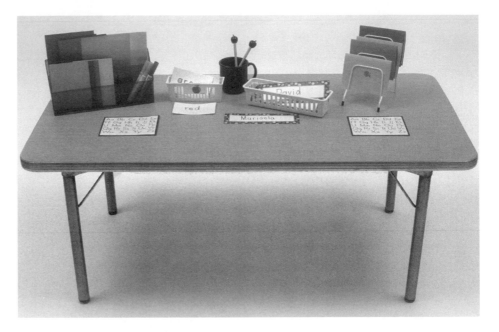

Description
Teachers often plan apple tasting, cooking experiences with apples, and apple printing in autumn. The apple writing center is designed to coordinate with other apple-related experiences in the classroom. The apple writing center offers opportunities for children to build on those experiences. They can read the color word cards for different types of apples and copy the words with a red, yellow, or green marker.

Child's Level
This center is most appropriate for preschool and kindergarten children.

Materials
- word cards, made by printing the words *red, yellow,* and *green* on individual 3-by-5-inch index cards (use a red, yellow, or light green marker to print the appropriate color word)
- markers—red, yellow, and light green
- name card with an apple border (available in some school-supply catalogs) for each child and teacher in the class
- apple pencils, one for each place at the center
- red, yellow, green, and white duplicating paper (half- and quarter-sheets)
- blank books with apple illustration, duplicated on red, yellow, and green paper

◆ containers to hold pencils, paper, blank books, word cards, and name cards

What to Look For
Children will experiment with the pencils and markers.
Some children may initially attempt to write on the word or name cards. They can be directed to use paper.
Children may read the color words.
Some children will attempt to copy the color words using either a pencil or the corresponding color marker.
Children may display different stages of writing, from random scribble to conventional letter formation.

Modifications
After one week, add a fill-in-the-blank paper, *I like _____ apples best*. Children may wish to copy the color word of their favorite type of apple. The fill-in will be the most intriguing after children have tasted different apples and perhaps voted for their favorite one.
Print the color words using a black marker and add a picture cue, made with red, yellow, and green apple stickers.

Comments & Questions to Extend Thinking
Which is your favorite apple?
Would you like to use the apple pencil or the red marker to write the word "red"?
See if you can find the word "green."
Kate wants to sit by me at lunch. Can you help her find my name card?
Can you find a color word that has two letters that are exactly the same?

Comments & Questions to Encourage Phonetic Awareness
I hear the sound for the letter "o" at the end of yellow, but the word really ends with a "w."
There are two "e's" in "green," but I can only hear the sound for one "e." Two "e's" go together to make a long "e" sound.

Integrated Curriculum Activities
Set up the dramatic play area as a farmer's market, with small grocery bags or baskets, a cash register, and varieties of produce, including three types of apples.
Include the book *Apples and Pumpkins,* by Anne and Lizzy Rockwell, in the book area (New York: Scholastic, 1989).
Plan an apple tasting activity. Let children vote for their favorite apple and graph the results (see *More Than Counting,* activity 6.5).

Helpful Hint

An apple sticker or rubber stamp can be used to add a context cue on the fill-in papers.

5.3 Autumn Changes

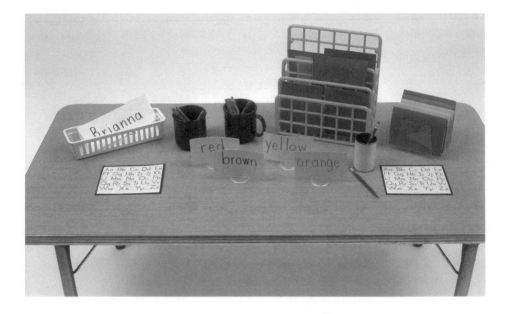

Description
Young children notice the changes in the environment during autumn. Teachers often include autumn songs, poems, and books in the curriculum materials during this seasonal change. These activities provide a foundation for this autumn writing center. Teachers might want to set up the autumn writing center after the apple center has been in the classroom for two or three weeks. The materials in both centers emphasize color words; however, the autumn center focuses on the changing colors of leaves and coordinates well with autumn songs about leaves.

Child's Level
This writing center is appropriate for preschool and kindergarten children. Modifications to the center increase the complexity of the writing activities for first-grade children.

Materials
- word cards, made by printing the words *red, yellow, orange,* and *brown* on individual 3-by-5-inch index cards (use red, yellow, orange, and brown markers to print the appropriate color words)
- red, yellow, orange, and brown colored pencils (two sets)
- red pencils, decorated with several autumn leaf stickers
- red, yellow, orange, brown, and white duplicating paper (half- and quarter-sheets)

- blank books, made with a leaf sticker or rubber stamp impression of a leaf on the original and duplicated on red, yellow, and orange paper
- name card for each child in the class (see activity 5.1 for instructions)
- containers, to hold the pencils, paper, and word cards

What to Look For

Children will experiment with reading the color word cards.

Children will copy the color words using the pencil or colored pencils.

Children may display different stages of writing, from random scribble to conventional letter formation.

Some children will recognize some of the color words based on their previous experiences with the apple writing center.

Modifications

Include paper cutouts shaped like leaves for more experienced children.

Print the color words in black ink, eliminate the picture, or place the picture cue on the back of the word card. Older children can verify the accuracy of their reading of the words. A small colored leaf sticker or dot of color provides the necessary context cue.

Comments & Questions to Extend Thinking

We collected leaves on the nature walk. What color of leaves did you find?

"Orange" starts with an "o." Look. It's a circle. Can you make a round mark for the "o"?

Comments & Questions to Encourage Phonetic Awareness

One of the color words begins with the same letters as "Grant." Can you find that word?

"Brown" and "green" both end with the letter "n." Listen for the sound at the end of each word as I say them. (Emphasize the final consonant.)

Sherein's name rhymes with "green." Can you think of any other words that rhyme with "green"?

Integrated Curriculum Activities

Sing autumn songs (see *More Than Singing*, activities 2.5 and 6.3).

Create an autumn art area (see *More Than Painting*, activity 2.6).

Helpful Hint

Do not display colored pencils in the art area at the same time or children may be confused and take them from area to area.

5.4 Colorful Mice Writing Center

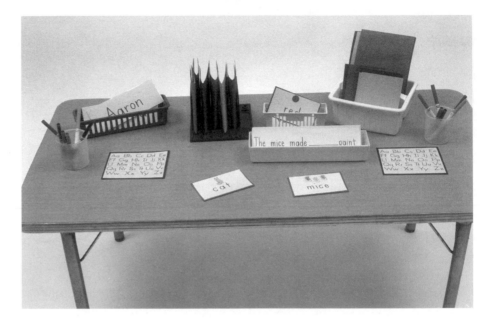

Description

Children love to mix colors in art activities. This center builds on that interest and includes a wider variety of color words than either the Apple or the Autumn writing center. The Colorful Mice writing center also coordinates well with the book *Mouse Paint*, by Ellen Stoll Walsh (New York: Harcourt, 1989). In the story, tiny white mice get into paint pots and mix primary colors together. The *mice, cat,* and color word cards and fill-in papers encourage children to think more about color combinations as well as to retell the story of the mice in the book.

Child's Level

This writing center is appropriate for older preschool, kindergarten, and first-grade children. The center includes a larger number of word cards and accessories, which may be overwhelming to younger children. The modifications listed below would make this center more appropriate for less-experienced groups of children.

Materials

♦ word cards, made by printing the words *cat, mice, red, yellow, blue, green, orange,* and *purple* on individual 3-by-5-inch index cards
♦ self-adhesive paper circles (¾ inch) in each of the six colors
♦ sticker or rubber-stamp impressions of a cat and three mice

- two sets of colored pencils (red, yellow, blue, orange, green, and purple)
- red, yellow, orange, green, purple duplicating paper, and blue construction paper (half and quarter sheets)
- name card for each child in the class (see activity 5.1 for instructions)
- blank books with red, yellow, blue, green, orange, and purple covers
- fill-in-the-blank papers: for example, *The mice made _____ paint.*
- containers, for holding the pencils, paper, blank books, word cards, and name cards

What to Look For

Children will experiment with the materials at the writing center.

Children may display different stages of writing, from random scribble to conventional letter formation.

Some children will want to write in each color of book; others will have a favorite color.

Modifications

Eliminate the *cat* and *mice* word cards for younger children.

Add the fill-in papers after one or two weeks.

The board book version of *Mouse Paint* can be included at the writing center.

Comments & Questions to Extend Thinking

How did the mice hide from the cat in the story?

What happened after the mice mixed the colors together?

Which of these colors is your favorite?

Help Doug find the word card for "green." He wants to write it in his green book.

Comments & Questions to Encourage Phonetic Awareness

Which of the color words begins with the same sound as "paint"?

One of the words rhymes with Ted's name. Can you find that word?

Integrated Curriculum Activities

Include color-mixing activities in the art curriculum (see *More Than Painting*, activities 4.6, 5.9, 5.13, 5.16, 8.1, and 8.8).

Read the big-book version of *Mouse Paint* at group time, using the puppets that coordinate with the book. These are available in bookstores and catalogs.

Include other books about color, such as *Color Dance*, by Ann Jonas (New York: Greenwillow, 1989) and *Little Blue and Little Yellow*, by Leo Lionni (New York: Astor-Honor, 1993).

Helpful Hint

Cut the blue construction paper the same size as the duplicating paper.

5.5 Alphabet Writing Center

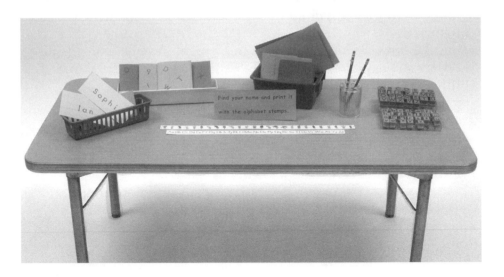

Description

Many children recognize the uppercase letters of the alphabet as well as the lowercase letters with the same formation, such as *C/c*, *X/x*, and *W/w*. This writing center builds on children's interest in the alphabet book *Chicka Chicka Boom Boom*, by Bill Martin Jr. and John Archambault (New York: Simon & Schuster, 1989), and provides models for the complete alphabet. The alphabet rubber stamps also provide opportunities for children who may be less comfortable writing or may not yet have the finger strength to print in a more conventional form.

Child's Level

This writing center is appropriate for preschool children and for kindergarten children at the beginning of the school year. The materials are also very beneficial for children with physical disabilities, who may be able to copy their names or write messages even if they cannot do those things with a pencil.

Materials

- name card for each child and teacher in the class, made by printing each name on sentence strips using the alphabet rubber stamps
- bright colors of duplicating or construction paper (half- and quarter-sheets), to match the book
- blank books, made by printing a variety of alphabet rubber-stamp impressions on the original and duplicating on bright colors to match the book
- colorful pencils with an alphabet eraser secured near the top

Helpful Hint

Use superglue to adhere the alphabet eraser to the pencil. Hot glue does not work.

- rubber alphabet stamps, both upper- and lowercase
- sign for the wall, *Find your name and print it with the rubber stamps.*
- containers, for holding the pencils, paper, blank books, word cards, and name cards

What to Look For

Children will eagerly read the novel name cards.

Children may print their names with the rubber stamps or attempt to print their names at a developmentally appropriate level of writing.

Some children may write messages in the blank books using the rubber stamps.

Younger, less-experienced children may experiment with the rubber stamps rather than attempt to copy names or write messages.

Modifications

For very young children, limit the selection of alphabet stamps to uppercase letters only. In some cases, teachers might want to display only the first letter of each child's name.

The board book *Chicka Chicka ABC* can be included at the writing center.

Comments & Questions to Extend Thinking

Can you find a stamp for the first letter in your name?

Look: You have to make an "f" imprint twice to write "Jeff."

Use the capital letter (this one) for the first letter in your name.

Comments & Questions to Encourage Phonetic Awareness

Which letters are needed for the sounds in your name?

Let's say each sound as you stamp your name.

Integrated Curriculum Activities

Make the alphabet interactive chart to include in the music or other area of the classroom (activity 3.6).

Include alphabet puzzles in the curriculum.

Make an alphabet memory game for the class (activity 6.3).

5.6 Winter Writing Center

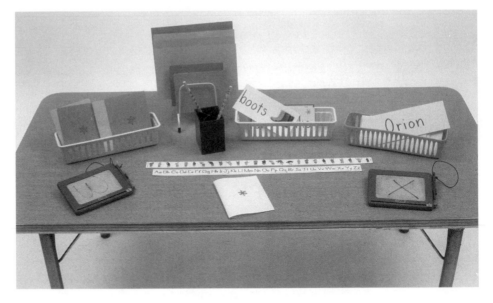

Description

Snow and snowmen intrigue and fascinate many young children. Scarves, mittens, and boots are part of the everyday winter experience for many children. This writing center coordinates with their interest in seasonal changes.

Child's Level

This winter writing center is most appropriate for preschool and kindergarten children, during a period of cold, snowy weather.

Materials

- ◆ word cards, made by printing the words *snowflake, snowman, mittens, gloves, scarf,* and *boots* on individual white sentence strips
- ◆ stickers, rubber-stamp impressions, or illustrations for each of the word cards
- ◆ name card for each child in the class (see activity 5.1 for instructions)
- ◆ several shades of blue duplicating paper (half- and quarter-sheets)
- ◆ snowflake pencils
- ◆ blank books, made with a snowflake or snowman illustration on the original, and duplicated on shades of blue paper
- ◆ containers, to hold the pencils, paper, blank books, name cards, and word cards

What to Look For

Children will talk about snow and snowmen as they use the
  writing center materials.

Children will experiment with copying the word cards.

Children will demonstrate various stages of development, from
  random scribble to conventional letter formation.

Some children may read the word cards.

Some children may want the teacher to write messages or descriptions of winter experiences in the blank books.

Older children may wish to create their own word cards with a
  picture of the item and the word.

Modifications

Add rubber stamps for some of the winter items.

Add paper cutouts shaped like mittens.

Comments & Questions to Extend Thinking

We have had a lot of snow. Do you wear gloves or mittens when it
  is cold?

I like to make snowmen. Have you read the book *Snowballs* yet?

What do you want to write in your book?

Comments & Questions to Encourage Phonetic Awareness

I hear the sound for the letter "s" at the end of some words and at
  the beginning of others. Listen as I say each word—"snowflake,"
  "snowman," "mittens," "gloves," and "boots."

What sound do you hear at the beginning of the word "mitten"?

Becky wants to write "snow." Look: The "o" and "w" go together to
  make a long "o" sound.

Integrated Curriculum Activities

Include books such as *The Jacket I Wear in the Snow*, by Shirley
  Neitzel (New York: Greenwillow, 1989); *Snowballs*, by Lois
  Ehlert (San Diego: Harcourt, 1995); *In the Snow*, by Huy Voun
  Lee (New York: Holt, 1995); and *Snow on Snow on Snow*, by
  Cheryl Chapman (New York: Dial, 1994).

Sing songs about snow and winter (see *More Than Singing*, activities 2.6 and 6.6).

Put snow, buckets, and shovels in the sensory table.

Place the interactive chart "Snowflakes Are Swirling" in the music
  area with finger cymbals (activity 3.3).

Create winter math games (see *More Than Counting*, activities
  3.16, 4.11, 4.16, 5.10, and 5.21).

Design a winter art area (see *More Than Painting*, activity 2.7).

Helpful Hints

Picture cues made with
rubber stamps will be
more appealing if they
are decorated with
colored pencils.

Children's clothing
catalogs are a good
resource for illustra-
tions of boots, mittens,
and gloves.

5.7 Bakery Writing Center

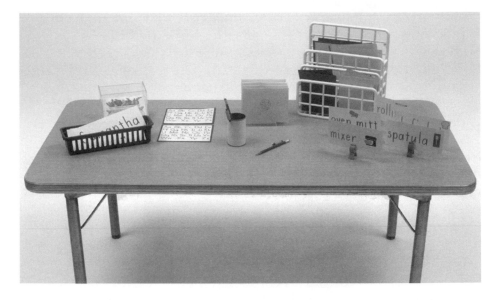

Description

This writing center coordinates with a dramatic play area set up as a bakery, with aprons, pot holders, cookie sheets, and play food, such as loaves of bread, pretzels, bagels, and pita bread. The writing materials could also be set up in the dramatic play area as an alternative writing center.

Child's Level

This writing center is appropriate for preschool, kindergarten, and first-grade children. The selection of materials can be adjusted to the children's developmental levels to create a simple or very complex writing center.

Materials

- word cards, made by printing words such as *spoon, spatula, oven mitt, chef's hat, pan, bowl, apron, cookies,* and *bread* on individual recipe cards
- illustrations of the items used for word cards
- name card for each child in the class (see activity 5.1 for instructions)
- several shades of brown duplicating or construction paper (half- and quarter-sheets)
- red pencils, with small rolling pins attached to them with hot glue
- index cards or paper cut to look like recipe cards
- blank books, with stickers of bakery items or an illustration of cookies on the original, duplicated on white, yellow, and buff paper

- containers, to hold the pencils, papers, blank books, name cards, and word cards

What to Look For
Children will read the name and word cards.
Some children will copy the name and word cards.
Children may generate a list of bakery items by writing them on the blank books.
A few children may take the pencils and paper to the dramatic play area set up like a bakery.

Modifications
Add order forms to encourage children to generate a list of bakery foods to buy.
Include more word cards for older, more experienced children.
Add small slates or wipe-off boards. Children can create lists of words on them.

Comments & Questions to Extend Thinking
What would you like to buy at the bakery?
What kinds of cookies did Mr. Cookie Baker make? (See Integrated Curriculum activities, below.)
I want to order a cake. Can you write my order down?

Comments & Questions to Encourage Phonetic Awareness
What do you think this word says? It starts with a "c." (Cover the picture cue.)
I want to write the word "cookie." What sound do you hear at the beginning? What letter should I write?
What sounds do you hear in "pie"?

Integrated Curriculum Activities
Set up the dramatic play area as a bakery.
Plan a field trip to a local bakery, purchase a loaf of bread, and make sandwiches at school.
Plan cooking activities, such as making soft pretzels, cookies, and bread.
Include books, such as *The Doorbell Rang*, by Pat Hutchins (New York: Greenwillow, 1986); *Mr. Cookie Baker*, by Monica Wellington (New York: Dutton, 1992); and *Jake Baked a Cake*, by B. G. Hennessy (New York: Viking, 1990).
Let the children estimate how many cookies will fit in a cookie jar (see *Much More Than Counting*, activity 3.7).
Use magnetic cookies with a cookie sheet divided into boxes with plastic tape (see *Much More Than Counting*, 1.1).

Helpful Hint
A recipe box can be used to hold the index cards or recipe cards.

5.8 Pizza Writing Center

Description
Pizza is a favorite food of many young children. This pizza writing center encourages children to consider all kinds of toppings for pizza. They can experiment with writing several words with double vowels or consonants, such as *cheese, green pepper, mushrooms,* and *pepperoni.*

Child's Level
This writing center is most appropriate for preschool and kindergarten children.

Materials
- word cards for pizza toppings, such as cheese, pepperoni, tomatoes, sausage, mushrooms, and green peppers
- illustrations of the toppings used for word cards
- name card for each child in the class (see activity 5.1 for instructions)
- red, yellow, or brown pencils, with a few pizza stickers on each one for decoration
- red, yellow, and white duplicating paper (half- and quarter-sheets)
- paper cut into a circle, stored in an individual-size pizza box
- empty spice jar, as pictured above, to hold the pencils
- containers, to hold the paper, the name cards, and the word cards

Illustrations for pizza toppings can be found on boxes of frozen pizza.

Computer clip art might also include pictures of the ingredients.

What to Look For

Children will recognize and read the word cards for pizza toppings, especially after they have voted for their favorite toppings.

Children will copy the word cards.

Some children may compare the word cards at the writing center to the word cards for the Pizza interactive chart (see activity 3.9).

Children may write orders for pizza at a developmentally appropriate stage, from random scribble to conventional letter formations.

Some children may ask the teacher to assist them as they read or write.

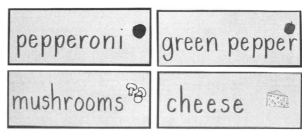

Modifications

Add blank books made with a pizza illustration on the original and duplicated on red, yellow, and white paper.

After one week, add a fill-in, *I like _____ best on pizza.*

Comments & Questions to Extend Thinking

What was the first thing we did when we made pizzas at school?

What is your favorite pizza topping?

Have you been to the pizza restaurant in the dramatic play area yet?

I like mushrooms on my pizza. Help me find that word card.

Comments & Questions to Encourage Phonetic Awareness

Listen as I say "pizza" and "pepperoni." Can you hear the same sound at the beginning of each word?

What pizza topping rhymes with the word "sneeze"? Can you think of any other words that rhyme with "sneeze"?

Look: The two "e's" go together in cheese to make a long "e" sound.

Integrated Curriculum Activities

Set up the dramatic play area as a pizza restaurant, with aprons, cash registers, pizza boxes, menus, and order forms.

Include an interactive chart that incorporates pizza toppings as the key words (activity 3.9).

Plan a field trip to a local pizza restaurant to eat pizza.

Make pizzas as a cooking activity and eat them for snack.

Include the book *Hi, Pizza Man,* by Virginia Walters (New York: Orchard, 1995), in the reading area.

Clap the syllables of pizza toppings as a rhythm activity (see *More Than Singing,* activity 3.13).

5.9 Construction Zone Writing Center

Description
Children enjoy pretending to fix things. Many early childhood programs include woodworking activities in the curriculum. This writing center includes word cards for tools associated with construction.

Child's Level
This writing center is appropriate for both preschool and kindergarten children.

Materials
- word cards for tools, such as hammer, saw, screwdriver, and pliers
- stickers or illustrations of the tools used for the word cards
- name card for each child in the class (see activity 5.1 for instructions)
- yellow pencils
- red, yellow, green, orange, and white duplicating paper (half- and quarter-sheets)
- blank books, made with clip art or a sticker of a hammer, saw, or other tool on the original, and duplicated on red, yellow, green, and orange paper
- containers, to hold the pencils, paper, blank books, name cards, and word cards

Helpful Hint

An inexpensive toothbrush holder can be used for displaying the pencils.

What to Look For

Children will copy the word cards into the blank books.

Children will begin to recognize and read the words for tools.

Many children will read the names of the other children in the class.

Children will demonstrate a range of development in writing, from random scribble to conventional letter formations.

Modification

Substitute construction vehicle word cards, such as *backhoe, front loader, dump truck,* and *crane* in place of the tool word cards.

Use stickers or clip art for the picture cues on the word cards.

Blank books can be made with the same illustrations.

Comments & Questions to Extend Thinking

Which of these tools are in the dramatic play area?

What tool would I need to cut wood?

Help me find the "hammer" word card.

Comments & Questions to Encourage Phonetic Awareness

What sound do you hear at the beginning of "hammer"? An "h" makes that sound.

What sounds do you hear in "saw"? The "a" and "w" go together to make a sound.

Integrated Curriculum Activities

Set up the dramatic play area as a construction site, with flannel shirts, hard hats, pretend tools, measuring tapes, and blueprints.

Include books such as *Building a House,* by Byron Barton (New York: Greenwillow, 1981), and *The Toolbox,* by Anne and Harlow Rockwell (New York: Macmillan, 1971), in the dramatic play area.

Create construction math games (see *Much More Than Counting,* activities 6.8, 7.8a, and 7.8b).

5.10 Spring Writing Center

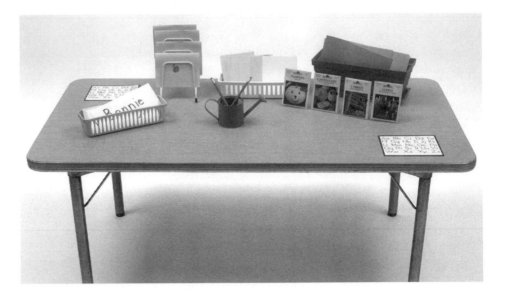

Description
Spring is a period of new growth outdoors. During this time many programs for young children include planting activities in the curriculum. This spring writing center coordinates well with planting activities and books, such as *The Carrot Seed,* by Ruth Krauss (New York: Harper, 1995).

Child's Level
This writing center is most appropriate for preschool and kindergarten children. Modifications to the center will create a more complex area for first-grade children.

Materials
- word cards made from empty seed packets for a variety of flowers or vegetables, such as *rose, daisy, pansy, bean, carrot,* and *lettuce* (reseal the packets and laminate)
- name card for each child in the class (see activity 5.1 for instructions)
- green pencils
- pastel shades of duplicating paper (half- and quarter-sheets)
- small watering can, to hold the pencils
- rectangular plastic flower pot, to hold the paper
- blank books, with an illustration of flowers or vegetables on the original, duplicated on pastel shades of paper
- containers, to hold the blank books, name cards, and word cards

What to Look For

Children will experiment with copying the word cards.

Some children will want to copy all of the word cards into a blank book.

Some children will illustrate their books.

Children will demonstrate a range of development in writing, from random scribble to conventional letter formations.

Some children will delight in adding the names of friends, family members, or the teacher to the fill-in papers.

Modifications

Include a fill-in-the-blank paper with _____ said, *"It won't come up."*

For older children, add seed catalogs and order forms. They can create a shopping list by copying names from the catalog.

Replace the seed packets with word cards for the flower and vegetable names. Place the picture on the back of the word card or eliminate it for first-grade children.

Comments & Questions to Extend Thinking

Choose your favorite flower. You can write it in this book.

Look. The word "sunflower" has two words put together: "sun" and "flower."

Which vegetable word do you want to write?

Comments & Questions to Encourage Phonetic Awareness

What's the first sound you hear in "carrot"? A "k" or a "c" can make that sound. This time it's a "c."

James wants to buy some corn seeds. Do you think "corn" begins with a "c" like carrot or a "k" like "kale"? Let's check the seed packet label.

Integrated Curriculum Activities

Set up the dramatic play area as a garden store, with aprons, cash register, small flowerpots and artificial flowers, empty seed packets, small garden tools, and seed catalogs.

Place potting soil, empty flowerpots, small shovels, and artificial flowers in the sensory table.

Plant a variety of seeds in one flat and observe the growth of the plants.

Plan a field trip to a garden store to purchase seeds or plants to plant at school.

Make a path game based on planting (see *More Than Counting*, activity 5.19 and 5.8).

Create a spring art center (see *More Than Painting*, activity 2.8).

Helpful Hint

Inexpensive seed packets can be found at closeout stores.

5.11 Grocery Store Writing Center

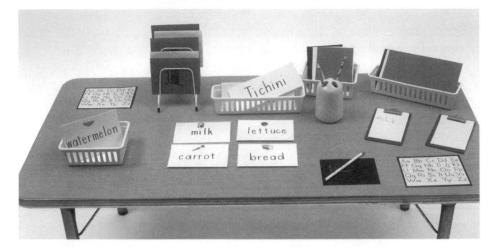

Description

Most young children accompany their parents to the grocery store and may enjoy selecting a specific cereal or cookies to purchase. This writing center coordinates well with a dramatic play area set up as a grocery store and the book *Feast for Ten*, by Cathryn Falwell (New York: Clarion, 1993). In the story a family shops for groceries and returns home to cook a feast. Children enjoy making grocery lists and experimenting with the white-colored pencil on black paper.

Child's Level

This writing center is appropriate for preschool, kindergarten, and first-grade children. Some modifications might be made for younger children if the quantities of materials are overwhelming.

Materials

- word cards of grocery items such as *cereal, milk, soap, macaroni and cheese, banana, apple, orange,* and so on
- stickers or illustrations of the groceries used for the word cards
- name card for each child in the class (see activity 5.1 for instructions)
- red, white, and black duplicating or construction paper (half- and quarter-sheets)
- blank books made with a clip-art illustration of a grocery cart on the original and duplicated on red and white paper
- fancy pencils, such as silver or gold, and white colored pencils
- containers, to hold the pencils, paper, word cards, and name cards

What to Look For

Children will recognize and read the word cards, especially after they have played in the dramatic play area.

Children will copy the word cards.

Some children may compare the word cards at the writing center to the actual boxes and cans of food in dramatic play.

Some children may write grocery lists, at a developmentally appropriate stage, from random scribble to conventional letter formations.

Some children may want to write words not found on the word cards.

Children will experiment with the white pencils and black paper.

Modifications

Add more word cards for older, more experienced children.

Include inexpensive notepads for making shopping lists.

Add small slates or wipe-off boards. Children can create grocery lists on them.

Add tracing paper, box fronts, and labels from cans. Older children may want to trace the print.

Comments & Questions to Extend Thinking

What groceries should we write on our shopping list?

Can you help me find the word card for "apples"? I like to eat them.

This book is full of writing, Dwayne. Help me read what you wrote.

Comments & Questions to Encourage Phonetic Awareness

Listen to the beginning of "cereal." This time the "s" sound is made by a "c."

Let's write all the sounds in "soap." Look at the word card. The "o" and "a" go together to make the long "o" sound.

What sound does "apple" start with? An "a" makes that sound.

Integrated Curriculum Activities

Set up the dramatic play area as a grocery store, with aprons, cash registers, small bags or baskets, and a variety of grocery items.

Plan a field trip to a grocery store. Children can help generate the list of ingredients needed for a picnic lunch.

Create a math game with novelty foods and shopping carts to hold them (see *Much More Than Counting*, activity 5.12).

Helpful Hint

Coupons are an excellent source of illustrations for the word cards.

5.12 Baby Writing Center

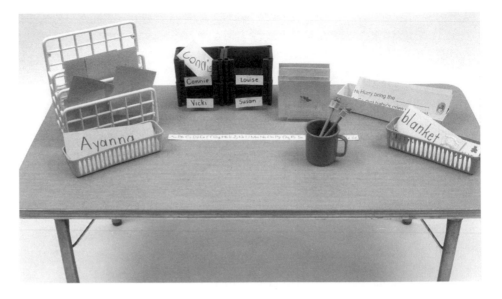

Description

The baby writing center incorporates the familiar words associated with caring for babies and dolls. The same words are the key words used for the interactive chart, "Hurry Mama" (activity 3.11). Children may want to select items for the baby to complete the fill-in papers and write or dictate stories about themselves as babies.

Child's Level

This writing center is appropriate for both preschool and kindergarten children.

Materials

- word cards for *bottle, blanket, rattle,* and *teddy bear*
- stickers or illustrations of the items used for word cards
- name card for each child in the class (see activity 5.1 for instructions)
- blank books made with a sticker of a baby item on the original and duplicated on pastel paper
- pastel pencils
- pastel duplicating paper (half- and quarter-sheets)
- containers, to hold the pencils, paper, name cards, and word cards

Helpful Hint

If stickers are not available, wrapping paper may be a source for the word card illustrations.

What to Look For

Many children will have ideas to add to the fill-in papers.
Some children will want to talk or write about baby brothers or sisters.
Some children will compare the word cards to the "Hurry Mama" chart if it is also displayed in the classroom (activity 3.11).
Children will demonstrate a range of development in writing, from random scribble to standard letter formations.

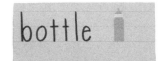

Modifications

After one week, add a fill-in paper, *Hurry, bring the ___ so that baby's cries won't last.*
Add other word cards, such as *diaper, rubber duck,* and *pacifier.*
Create blank book shaped liked baby items, such as bottles or booties.

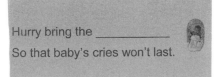

Comments & Questions to Extend Thinking

What baby items do you want to write in your book?
What do you think should go in the bottle for the baby?
Help me find the word card for "blanket."

Comments & Questions to Encourage Phonetic Awareness

I can think of two words with two "t's" in the middle. Can you figure out which words I'm thinking of?
"Bottle" and "blanket" both begin with a "b." Which word begins like "black"?
I hear two "buh" sounds in "baby." Listen as I say "baby."

Integrated Curriculum Activities

Set up the dramatic play area as a baby nursery, with extra dolls, doll clothes, blankets, rattles, bottles, and teddy bears.
Sing other baby songs (see *More Than Singing,* activities 2.1, 2.9, 2.12, and 2.13).
Make a class book to go with the song, "Hurry Mama." Each child completes a page in the books by selecting an item to bring to the baby to stop the crying (activity 4.4).
Use baby rattles at group time to accompany baby songs.
Play tapes of lullabies in many languages, such as those on the recording *The World Sings Goodnight* (Tom Wasinger, Boulder, CO: Silver Wave Records, 1993).

5.13 Summer Writing Center

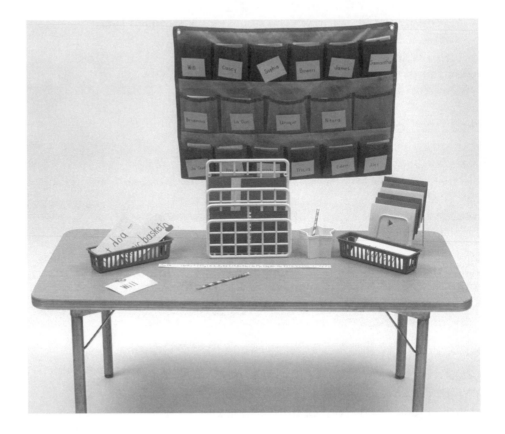

Description
Picnics are often associated with summer and warm weather. This center includes word cards with picnic items and encourages children to compile lists of items needed for a picnic.

Child's Level
This writing center is appropriate for preschool, kindergarten, and first-grade children.

Helpful Hint

Look for the pencils near the Fourth of July.

Materials
- word cards for *cooler, hot dog, hamburger, watermelon,* and *picnic basket*
- name card for each child in the class (see activity 5.1 for instructions)
- red, white, and blue paper (half- and quarter-sheets)
- blank books made with a sticker of a picnic item on the original and duplicated on red, white, and blue paper
- red, white, and blue striped pencils

- baskets for the blank books, name cards, and word cards
- star-shaped or other container for the pencils

What to Look For
Children will want to talk and write about their own picnic experiences.

Some children will copy all of the word cards into their books.

Some children will add other words to their books. They may use invented spelling, phonetic spelling, or look for them in a picture dictionary.

Older children may write in sentences.

Modifications
Add small notebooks to encourage children to make lists of picnic items.

Add other picnic or camping word cards, such as *tent, cooler,* and *sleeping bag.*

Comments & Questions to Extend Thinking
Let's make a list of what we need for a picnic. We can have a picnic outside later in the week.

I see "hot dog" in your book. Do you want to write "ketchup" to go with it?

Comments & Questions to Encourage Phonetic Awareness
I want to bring some lemonade on my picnic. Can you help me figure out how to spell that word?

Wesley says he saw an ant on a picnic. What letters does he need to write the sounds in "ant"?

Integrated Curriculum Activities
Add picnic items to the dramatic play area. Include towels or small tablecloths, small baskets, play food, and sunglasses.

Include the interactive chart "I Went Camping" in the curriculum (activity 3.5).

Include the book *One Hot Summer Day,* by Nina Crews (New York: Greenwillow, 1995), in the reading area.

5.14 Rhyming Writing Center

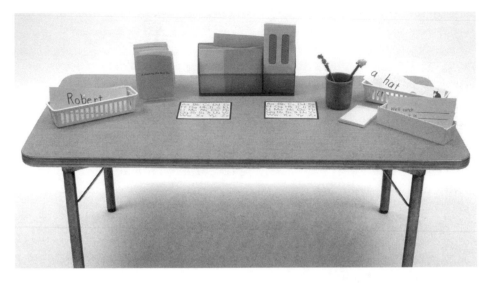

Description

Older preschool, kindergarten, and first-grade children are often fascinated with rhyming words. Experimenting with the sounds of the language and listening carefully for words that rhyme help children develop phonemic awareness. A writing center based on a song or book with rhyming words, such as the traditional song "Oh, A-Hunting We Will Go" (see activity 2.8 for the music), encourages children to compare how words that sound almost alike look when written. This writing center includes word cards with rhyming words from the song and also encourages children to create new rhymes to include in the song.

> Oh, a-hunting we will go, a-hunting we will go,
> We'll catch <u>a cat</u> and put him in <u>a hat</u>,
> And then we'll let him go.

> Additional rhymes:
> bear–chair; goat–coat; kitten–mitten;
> mole–hole; hen–pen; duck–truck

Child's Level

This writing center is most appropriate for older preschool, kindergarten, and first-grade children.

Materials

◆ word cards, for the rhyming words in the song
◆ illustrations, for the word cards

- index cards, for children to use to create their own rhyming words
- blank books, with the words "A-Hunting We Will Go" printed on the front
- pencils with lightweight animals on the tops
- baskets, for the blank books, name cards, and word cards
- fill-in-the-blank sheets that read, "We'll catch _____ and put it in _____."

What to Look For
Children will recite the words to the song and look for the printed form of the words.

Some children will locate word cards for the rhyming words.

Some children will look carefully at the rhyming words to see what letters are different.

Some children will make up new rhymes for the song. They may use phonetic spelling to write them.

Some children will copy the word cards onto the fill-in papers.

Modifications
Include a book version of the song in the writing area, such as *Oh, A-Hunting We Will Go,* by John Langstaff (New York: Macmillan, 1974).

Include a children's dictionary in the writing center. Children may wish to look up the spelling of new rhyming words.

Comments & Questions to Extend Thinking
I have a word card for "fox." Help me find the card for "box."

What word rhymes with "pig"?

Comments & Questions to Encourage Phonetic Awareness
What sound is different when we say "boat" and "goat"?

I want to put "bee" in my book. Help me think of a word that rhymes with it.

Look at "skunk" and "bunk." They both end with the same three letters.

Integrated Curriculum Activities
Create a big book based on the song "A Hunting We Will Go" (activity 2.8).

Read other books with a strong rhyme, such as *Silly Sally,* by Audrey Wood (New York: Harcourt, 1992).

Preprint the words to the song, but leave a blank space for the rhyming words. Each child can create a page for a class book.

Helpful Hint

Look for pencils with animal tops in party-supply stores.

Literacy-Based Games and Manipulative Materials

Adam carefully placed each letter from an alphabet puzzle back into the frame. After he finished, he examined the puzzle and then selected several letters, which he placed on the floor to form the word dog. *Adam proudly read the word he had created. The teacher was surprised. Adam had significant speech delays and only spoke in single words or two-word phrases, yet clearly he was advanced in his understanding of the printed word.*

▲ ▲ ▲

Mandy experimented with placing foam letters onto a Plexiglas easel in the water table. She dipped each letter into the water before sticking it onto the glass. Then she began to regroup the letters. She put all of the m's *together and then began to look for the* a's. *The teacher noted that Mandy grouped both upper- and lowercase* m's *together.*

▲ ▲ ▲

Children are surrounded by letters and words in their everyday world, so they are naturally curious about them. Literacy-based manipulative materials allow children to handle letters, rearrange them, and observe the results. As children play with letters and words, they construct important concepts about written language.

Teachers' Questions

Why is it important to include literacy-based manipulatives in classrooms?

Literacy-based manipulative materials and games help children become aware of letters and their relationship to words. As they play with literacy games and manipulative activities, children become familiar with letter shapes and forms. They learn to distinguish letters from other symbols and, with adult support, begin to identify specific letters. Children apply concepts of same, different, and similar to letter associations and form letter–word and letter–sound relationships.

What are some traditional literacy-based manipulative materials?

Letter puzzles and templates are the most common literacy-related manipulative materials in early childhood classrooms. They allow children to handle physical representations of letters and feel their outlines. If these are the only manipulative materials related to literacy available, however, children often lose interest in them. By including a variety of literacy-based games and manipulative materials in their classrooms, teachers stimulate children's interest and provide opportunities for them to construct a wide range of literacy relationships.

What kinds of manipulative materials can teachers design to encourage literacy development?

Letter and word games, materials with movable letters, and manipulative pieces used to extend stories all contribute to various aspects of literacy development. Letter games such as Letter Memory (activity 6.3) and Alphabet Bingo (activity 6.8) help children recognize and classify letters as a group of symbols, while word games such as Grab Bag (activity 6.5) and Add an E (activity 6.7) help them construct the relationship between letters and words. Movable alphabets encourage word play, which helps children further understand letter–word relationships. They learn that not every combination of letters results in a word, and that a specific set and sequence of letters is needed to produce a given word. Magnetic Words (activity 6.6) and Letter Tray (activity 6.9) are examples. Manipulative materials that are extensions of favorite stories or books promote reading comprehension and additional literacy skills, such as recognizing characters and story sequences. Story extensions might include flannelboard pieces (activity 6.16), puppets (activity 6.18), or manipulative pieces (activity 6.19).

What should teachers consider when making literacy games?

The games should have correctly formed letters and be attractive and durable. Clear and accurate printing is essential since the games provide a print model, and young children have difficulty recognizing letters that are crooked or not correctly formed. Appendix B includes a standard print model, which teachers can copy if needed. Children are attracted to games that are neatly made and have pleasing illustrations or detail. Laminating the materials is the most aesthetically pleasing way to ensure durability, although a clear self-adhesive plastic coating, such as Con-Tact paper, can also be used.

What should teachers consider when introducing literacy-based manipulative materials?

The movable letters should be carefully arranged so children can easily locate the letters they are looking for. Divided trays, sewing or tackle boxes with drawers, and pocket holders are useful devices for organizing movable alphabets. See the activities in this chapter for organizational ideas related to specific materials.

What kinds of materials can teachers assemble or design for children to use as book extensions?

Teachers can create flannelboard pieces to coordinate with books, use puppets to re-enact stories, or assemble small manipulative pieces for children to use as story extensions. Story characters and props to place on flannelboards can be cut from paper and attached with Velcro-brand fastener fabric or cut from felt (activity 6.16). Children can use generic puppets or stuffed animals to dramatize various stories (activity 6.18) or specific character dolls that match favorite books. Party-supply or craft stores are good sources for small figures to represent the characters in many books (activity 6.19).

What should teachers consider when creating story extensions?

The manipulative pieces should resemble the story characters as closely as possible so that children can draw clear associations between the manipulative materials and the book they represent. For example, if a teacher decides to create manipulative pieces to coordinate with a popular book, and one of the characters is a purple cat, the teacher should include a purple cat with the manipulative pieces since children would probably not associate a non-purple cat with that particular book. This might necessitate coloring a white cat with a purple permanent marker. Any teacher-made materials used for story extensions should be attractive and durable.

How can teachers incorporate literacy-based manipulatives throughout the classroom?

Teachers can create manipulative activities to coordinate with songs in the music area, introduce waterproof literacy materials into the sensory table, and use art media in conjunction with literacy-based manipulative materials. Teachers might include a movable alphabet in the music area to spell prominent words in popular songs. Sponge letters to use as printing tools with paint (activity 6.13) and letter molds to use with playdough (activity 6.14) expand literacy development through art media. Foam letters, which adhere to flat surfaces in the water table, extend literacy into the sensory area (activity 6.12).

How should teachers display literacy-based manipulative materials?

Teachers should group all the component pieces of an activity so that children can immediately tell which materials belong together. A tray, basket, small bench, or section of a divided shelf can be used to organize all necessary materials for an activity. For example, letter beads mounted on a dowel might be used in conjunction with word cards (activity 6.10). Children can rotate the beads to form the words on the cards. Since both materials are essential parts of the activity, the teacher might display them together on a small tray so children can immediately tell that they go together.

How can teachers use manipulatives and literacy games to encourage phonetic awareness?

Teachers can design specific materials to highlight phonics concepts and discuss letter–sound relationships with children as they interact with materials. Children construct phonetic relationships by interacting with print and observing the sounds that correlate with specific letters or letter combinations. Teachers can design interesting games to highlight specific phonetic concepts for children who are developmentally ready (activity 6.7). Teachers can also point out letter–sound relationships incidentally as children experiment with literacy-based manipulative materials and games. For example, when children are playing a game such as alphabet bingo (activity 6.8), the teacher might emphasize the sound of each letter in addition to naming it. Each activity in this chapter includes suggestions for comments and questions to enhance phonetic awareness.

How can teachers assess children's literacy development with literacy games and manipulatives?

Teachers can use anecdotal records, photographs, or assessment forms to document children's literacy development. Through anecdotal notes, teachers can note what materials a child uses and what concepts emerge through their interactions. When playing literacy games with a child, the teacher may wish to use a quick, shorthand notation so that writing the anecdotal notes doesn't interrupt the flow of the game. Later, the notes can be transferred to a notebook, the child's portfolio, a computer file, or whatever data-organization system the teacher prefers.

Photographs can instantly capture literacy development. For example, if a child uses a movable alphabet to form words, a photograph of the child and what she creates with the letters preserves the data. Later, the photo can be included in the child's portfolio or a year-end scrapbook (activity 4.19).

Assessment forms can provide a quick way for teachers to organize literacy information. Sample forms are included in appendixes C and D.

Literacy-Based Games and Manipulative-Material Activities

Word Banks
Word Game

Description
Children seem to learn to read first the words that are interesting to them. For this activity, each child has a notebook ring to hold personal word cards. Each day children can add one new word of their choice to their individual word banks, if they wish.

Child's Level
This activity is appropriate for older preschool, kindergarten, or first-grade children.

Materials
- white 3-by-5-inch index cards, with a hole punched near the top of each card
- colored index cards, each with a child's name printed on it, for the fronts of the word banks
- attractive note paper, to decorate the fronts of the word banks (optional)
- notebook ring, to hold the cards

Helpful Hint

Teachers should write the words that go into the word banks so there is a clear print model for the children to read.

What to Look For
Children will select a wide variety of words for their word banks, including the names of television or movie characters.

Some children will at first guess at the words based on their initial letters.

Some children will begin to recognize the words from their word banks in other contexts.

Some children will not be able to read the words from their word banks but will gain a clearer understanding of the relationship between spoken and written language.

Modification

When a child has accumulated a substantial number of words, a sorting system may be helpful. (Usually only a few children get to this point.) At this point, you may offer the child the option of using a small file box with alphabet dividers, and filing the words by their initial letters.

Comments & Questions to Extend Thinking

What word would you like to add to your word bank today? Do you have a favorite toy or animal?

"Tyrannosaurus" is a long word. It stretches across the whole card.

You already have "snow" in your word bank. Can you find it? When I write "snowman," I have to first write "snow" and then add "m-a-n."

Comments & Questions to Encourage Phonetic Awareness

Listen to the beginning of "fox." An "f" makes that sound.

What sounds do you hear in "Batman?"

Listen to the beginning of "kitty" and "cat." They both start with the same sound, but a "k" makes that sound in "kitty" and a "c" makes that sound in "cat."

Integrated Curriculum Activities

Use words from the children's word banks to write individual books for them to read.

Create games that incorporate words from children's word banks (activities 6.2, 6.3, and 6.4).

Display the word banks in the class writing area so children can incorporate them into their writing.

Create a class word bank with words that are important to the whole class, such as words related to a group project or a popular curriculum topic.

6.2 Lucky Stars
Word Bank Game

Thanks to Jan Annett for this idea.

Description

This game incorporates words from children's word banks (activity 6.1). After a child accumulates ten words in his or her word bank, the words are copied onto star-shaped paper. The child places the stars face down, turns them over one at a time, and accumulates a point for each word read. The game can be taken home to share with the child's family. Since the words from the word bank have all been selected by the child, there is usually a high degree of interest in the game.

Child's Level

This game is most appropriate for older preschool, kindergarten, or first-grade children.

Helpful Hint

Cut out the stars well ahead of time. The games quickly become popular.

Materials

- ◆ construction paper, cut into star shapes (or whatever shape is desired by the child), with one word from the child's word bank printed on each star
- ◆ lamination (optional)
- ◆ small resealable bag, to hold the stars
- ◆ sheet with simple directions, for parents, such as the sample shown

What to Look For

Many children will remember the words from their word banks that are printed on the stars.

Some children will initially have trouble reading the words on the stars because they are in a different context from their word bank.

Some children will help other children read their words.

Children will eagerly await the tenth word in their word bank so they can acquire a Lucky Star game. This often leads to mathematical problem solving as they attempt to determine how many more words they need.

Modification

When children reach twenty words in their word banks, another game can be made for them, perhaps using a different shape of paper.

Comments & Questions to Extend Thinking

I turned over a word that starts with "m." Can you help me read it?

I see the word "fire" on both of these stars—"fire truck" and "fire fighter."

Can you help Nancy read this word?

Comments & Questions to Encourage Phonetic Awareness

What do you think this star says? It starts with a "b" sound.

You read this word as "Dan," and that's almost what it says. Look at the last letter. How would that "d" sound at the end? (Dad)

This word starts with the same sound as this one.

Send this note home to parents with the star game.

Integrated Curriculum Activities

Write books for each child using words from their individual word banks. They can then illustrate the books.

Display a magnetic board and letters along with the word banks. Children can form the words in their word banks with the magnetic letters.

Sing songs that focus on words and letters, such as "Bingo, Revisited" (see *More Than Singing,* activity 2.11). The children's names are substituted for *Bingo* in this reworking of the traditional song.

Lucky Star Game

This game has stars with words from your child's word bank. To play the game, turn the stars face down. The child picks the stars one at a time and reads the words. If the word is read correctly, the child gets a point. If you help with a word, you get a point. Continue through all the stars.

6.3 Letter Memory
Letter or Word Game

Description
This game allows children to match letters or words in a memory-game format. Either letters or words are printed on colored index cards, depending on the children's developmental stages. Children place the index cards face down and turn over two at a time. If they make a match, they keep the pair. If the cards do not match, they are again placed face down, and the next child takes a turn. Teachers can make memory games for individual children by using the words from their word banks (activity 6.1).

Child's Level
This activity is appropriate for older preschool, kindergarten, or first-grade children.

Materials
- colored 3-by-5-inch index cards
- press-on letters (optional)
- laminating materials (optional)

What to Look For
Children will look more carefully at the letters or words as they attempt to match the cards.

Children will help one another read the cards.

Some children will want to turn over all of the cards as they look for matches.

Some children will remember the placement of the cards and quickly make matches.

Helpful Hint
Be sure to use index cards that are all the same color. Otherwise, children may attempt to match the colors of the cards rather than focusing on the letters or words.

Modifications

Start with capital letters on the cards for younger children. They are easier to distinguish than lowercase letters.

For older or more experienced children, write words on the cards instead of letters. Select the words based on the interest and reading level of the children.

Comments & Questions to Extend Thinking

Turn over another card and see if it matches this one.

Alex thinks these two words match. They do look almost alike, but look at the last letter. "Car" ends with an "r" and "cat" ends with a "t."

Who can help Tara read this word?

Comments & Questions to Encourage Phonetic Awareness

Here's an "s." Sophie's name starts with that sound.

What do you think this word (bee) says? Look at the first letter. It makes a "buh" sound. The two "e's" together make this sound— "ee."

Integrated Curriculum Activities

Put a basket of magnetic letters on the manipulative shelf along with the memory game. Some children may wish to use the movable letters to spell the words.

Introduce other types of memory games, perhaps using pictures of animals or photographs of the children, as a precursor to this game.

Include alphabet books in the reading area.

6.4 My Words
Word Bank Path Game

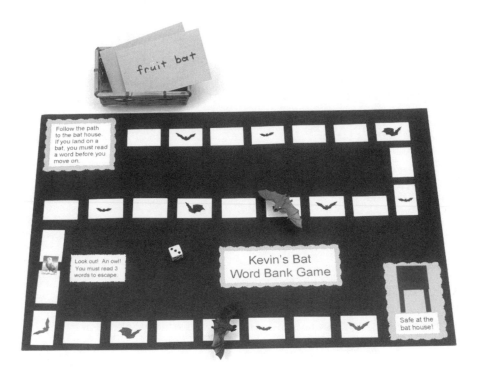

Description

When children have accumulated a given number of words in their word banks, teachers can make individual path games for them using their word bank words. Any child landing on a marked space attempts to read a word from the word bank of the child who owns the game. Children can help formulate the rules. The themes of the games should vary based on the interest of each child.

Child's Level

This game is appropriate for older preschool, kindergarten, or first-grade children.

Materials

◆ poster board, 14 by 22 inches
◆ 1½-inch-diameter white stickers or Post-It brand notes, for the path
◆ additional stickers, cutouts, or pictures, to illustrate the game board
◆ special sticker or symbol, to indicate that a word must be read

Helpful Hint

Mark lots of the path spaces with whatever symbol you have designated to indicate that a word must be read. This increases opportunities for reading.

- 3-by-5-inch index cards, to write the word-bank words on
- die
- several small figures, for movers

What to Look For
Children will be very excited to have their own game.
Children will have renewed interest in their word-bank words as they help other children try to read them.

Modification
Create additional word cards to add to the games as children accumulate more words in their word banks.

Comments & Questions to Extend Thinking
I landed on a bat. Can you help me read this word?
What rules do you want to make up for your game?
Look at the first letter in the word. That might help you remember what the word says.
This must be a name. It starts with a capital letter.

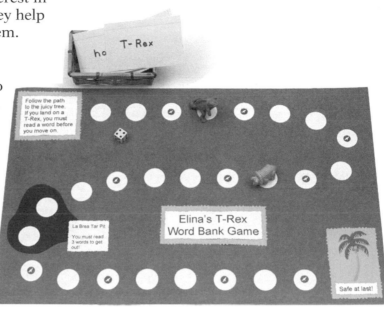

Comments & Questions to Encourage Phonetic Awareness
This word *(horse)* starts with an "h" sound. What sound does the "o-r" make?
Mark and Mary both have names that start with the same letter as this word. What sound do their names start with?

Integrated Curriculum Activities
Create a class game similar to the individual games, perhaps using words from a class word bank. When children take their own games home, there will still be one for the class to play.
Introduce other word games, such as "Add an E" (activity 6.7) and "Grab Bag" (activity 6.5).
Add foam letters to the sensory table (activity 6.12).

6.5 Grab Bag
Word Game

Description
For this game, wooden or plastic letters are placed in a small bag. Each player has a game board with several words printed on it. As the bag is passed around, players take turns drawing one letter at a time out of the bag. Then they try to match the letter to the letters on their board. Play continues until all the words have been spelled.

Child's Level
This activity is appropriate for older preschool, kindergarten, or first-grade children.

Materials
- 4 pieces of white poster board, approximately 6 by 8 inches each
- wooden or plastic letters
- dark pen or marker, to trace around the letters and form the words on the game boards
- stickers, to illustrate the words on the game boards
- small grab bag
- lamination or clear self-adhesive paper

What to Look For
Children will match the letters they draw from the bag to the letters on their boards.
Some children will gain a much better understanding of how letters go together to form words.

Helpful Hints

Trace around the wooden or plastic letters to create outlines for the letters on the game boards.

Be sure to have enough letters in the bag to spell all of the words. Several sets will probably be needed.

Some children will read the words on their boards.

Some children will remember how the words are spelled and write them in other contexts.

Modifications

Select shorter, easier words for younger or less experienced children.

For older children, use longer words on the game boards.

Comments & Questions to Extend Thinking

Can you find a place on your board where this letter will fit?

What letter do you need to draw to finish "dog" on your board?

Sanjay doesn't have a place to put the "t" he pulled out of the bag. What should he do with it?

Comments & Questions to Encourage Phonetic Awareness

Listen to the sound "a" makes in the word "cat" on your board.

You have the word "duck" on your board. What sound does "duck" start with?

Look at the end of "duck." The "c" and "k" go together to make a "kuh" sound.

Integrated Curriculum Activities

Put word cards that correspond to the words on the game boards in the writing area.

Use letter molds with playdough (activity 6.14).

Add wooden letter blocks (activity 6.11) to the manipulative area. Children may use the blocks to spell some of the words they remember from the game boards.

6.6 Magnetic Words
Word Game

Description
Magnetic letters are inexpensive and readily available. For this activity, children use magnetic letters to spell the words on teacher-made word cards.

Child's Level
This activity is most appropriate for older preschool and kindergarten children.

Materials
- several sets of lowercase magnetic letters
- magnetic board or cookie sheet on which to place the letters
- 3-by-5-inch index cards, with words of familiar objects or animals clearly printed on them
- stickers or small drawings, to illustrate the words

What to Look For
Children will look for letters to create the words on the cards.
Children will gain a better understanding of how letters go together to form words.
Some children will remember the spelling of certain words and write them in other contexts.

Helpful Hint
Use lowercase magnetic letters except for the first letters of names, since this is the way words are written in books.

Modification

Vary the words on the cards based on the interests of the children. For example, zoo animals might be appropriate for a class that is visiting the zoo.

Comments & Questions to Extend Thinking

What letters do you need for this word?

Look: You need two "e's" for "sheep."

"Cow" and "cat" both started with a "c."

Comments & Questions to Encourage Phonetic Awareness

Listen to the "a" in "cat." Now listen to the "a" in "snake." The "e" at the end of "snake" changes the sound of the "a."

What sound do the two "o's" together make in "zoo?"

Listen: "Shoe" starts with the same sound as "Sharon." The "s" and "h" go together to make a "shuh" sound.

Integrated Curriculum Activities

Put letter stamps in the writing area. Children can use them to create permanent representations of the words on the word cards.

Use the magnetic letters with letter books, such as *Chicka Chicka Boom Boom,* by Bill Martin Jr. and John Archambault (New York: Simon & Schuster, 1989). Children can use the letters to help tell the story.

Instead of word cards, use name cards with the magnetic letters. Children like to spell one another's names.

6.7 Add an E
Phonics Game

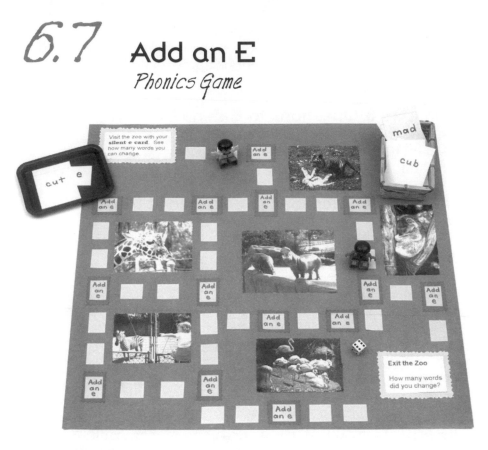

Description

This path game allows children to explore the effect of adding an *e* to the end of a short-vowel word. Each player has a small card with an *e* on it. As they advance along the path, they draw a word card each time they land on a space marked *add an e*. The word cards have short-vowel words, such as *hop*. After reading the word, the player adds his *e* card to the end of the word and reads the newly created long-vowel word. The beginning of the game reads, *Visit the zoo with your silent-e card. See how many words you can change*, while the end of the game reads, *How many words did you change?* This encourages children to read as many words as possible during the game.

Child's Level

This game is most appropriate for kindergarten or first-grade children.

Materials

- green poster board, 22 by 22 inches
- zoo stickers or pictures, to illustrate the game board
- yellow stickers or Post-It brand notes, 1 inch wide, for the path
- fine-line marker, to print the phrase *add an e* on some of the spaces

- red paper, for the borders around the *add an e* spaces
- 3-by-5-inch index cards, to write short-vowel words on
- several 1-inch-diameter squares cut from index cards, with *e* printed on each
- spinner or die
- several small figures, to use as playing pieces

What to Look For

Some children will be able to read the word cards.

Some children will at first need assistance reading the words.

Children will note the effect of adding an *e* to the end of a short-vowel word.

Some children will move around the game board without reading the words. They may use it as a math game.

Modification

Increase the number of words used in the game as children become more adept at reading them.

Comments & Questions to Extend Thinking

What does this word say? Listen to what happens when I put my "e" on the end.

Abby says she changed "pet" into "Pete" by putting an "e" on the end.

Will this word card still say "can" if I put an "e" on the end?

Comments & Questions to Encourage Phonetic Awareness

What sound does the "a" make in "tap?" What sound does it make after we put an "e" on the end of the word?

What happens to Sam's name when we put an "e" on the end? Does it still say "Sam"?

Put your "e" on your word card, and we'll read it again.

Integrated Curriculum Activities

Add a letter-bead twist game (activity 6.10) to the manipulative area. Children can create a variety of words by twisting the beads.

Use sponge letters with paint at the easel (activity 6.13). Children may wish to write words with them.

Helpful Hint

The following list of short-vowel words can be used for the word cards:

hop	van	can
far	mad	rag
dim	kit	win
ton	mop	not
cap	fat	man
rat	fin	pin
cub	rob	tot
car	hat	mat
pet	fir	rid
cut	rod	bar
fad	Jan	pan
bit	hid	rip
tub		

6.8 Alphabet Bingo
Letter Game

Description
This letter-bingo game is easy to make and endlessly popular. As the teacher holds up a card with a letter on it, the children look for the same letter on their boards and cover the letter with a bottle cap if they find it. The game encourages children to look carefully at the construction of letters as they attempt to make matches. Teachers facilitate the process by comparing letter formations, supplying letter names, and modeling letter and sound relationships.

Child's Level
This activity is most appropriate for preschool or kindergarten children.

Materials
◆ white paper, 7 by 6 inches, divided into twelve boxes with a dark marker and mounted on poster board (one board per player)
◆ 1-inch-tall stick-on letters
◆ colored bottle caps, for cover-up pieces (12 per board)
◆ white index cards, 3 by 5 inches, cut in half, with a letter mounted on each one
◆ small baskets, to hold the bottle caps
◆ laminating materials

Helpful Hint
The letters can be printed by hand or generated on a computer, if desired. Be sure the print is as close to a standard style as possible.

What to Look For

Children will match the letter the teacher holds up by covering the corresponding letter on their boards.

Some children will confuse letters that look similar, such as *K* and *F*.

Some children will name the letters.

Some children will think of words that start with particular letters, such as their names.

Modifications

Start with capital letters for children who are just beginning to play the game, since capital letters are easier for young children to distinguish.

Switch to lowercase letters once children are familiar with capital letters.

Comments & Questions to Extend Thinking

Can you find this letter on your board?

This is an "s." Who has a name that starts with "s" in our class?

What letters are left on your board to cover up?

Comments & Questions to Encourage Phonetic Awareness

This is a "d." It makes a "duh" sound, like "Daddy."

What letter is this? What sound do you think it makes?

Can you think of any words that start with this sound?

Integrated Curriculum Activities

Read a variety of alphabet books, such as *Navajo ABC*, by Luci Tapahonso (New York: Simon & Schuster, 1995); *A Is for Aloha*, by Stephanie Feeney (Honolulu: University Press of Hawaii, 1980); and *K Is for Kiss Goodnight*, by Jill Sardegna (New York: Bantam, 1994).

Put foam letters in the water table along with Plexiglas easels (activity 6.12).

Add letter stencils to the writing area (activity 6.15).

6.9 Letter Tray
Literacy Manipulative

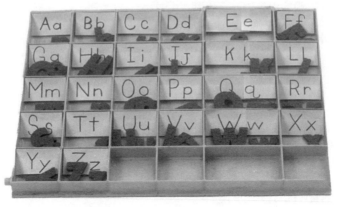

Description

Movable alphabets allow children to experiment with word construction and practice letter and word recognition. In this activity, wooden or plastic letters are organized on a divided tray for easier use. Word cards are included to encourage children to construct words with the letters.

Child's Level

This activity is most appropriate for older preschool or kindergarten children.

Materials

- divided tray or box, with 26 compartments, each clearly labeled with a capital letter and the corresponding lowercase letter
- plastic, wooden, or foam lowercase letters (include capital letters for the first letter in children's names)
- 3-by-5-inch index cards, with familiar words printed on them
- stickers, to illustrate the word cards
- recipe holder, to hold the word cards (optional)

What to Look For

Some children will sort the letters into their corresponding compartments.

Some children will use the letters to write words, such as their names.

Some children will use the letters to copy the word cards.

Some children will attempt to place the movable letters directly on top of the letters in the word cards.

Helpful Hint

Be sure there are enough letters available in the tray to copy all of the word cards. Children may want to line up all of the words that they have made.

Modification

Start with fewer letters for children who are younger or less experienced. Increase the number of letters as children become more adept at finding them in the tray.

Comments & Questions to Extend Thinking

What letters do you need to make this word?
I found a "t" on the floor. Where does it go in the tray?
What letter comes next in your word?

Comments & Questions to Encourage Phonetic Awareness

Look: You need a "b" for this "buh" sound in "baby," and then you need another "b" for this "buh" sound.
What sound does the "r" make at the beginning of "robot"?
Listen: "Mom" starts and ends with an "m" sound.

Integrated Curriculum Activities

Add word cards to the writing area (see chapter 5). Children may wish to write the same words they have formed with the movable alphabet.
Use sponge letters with paint to create letters and words in another medium (activity 6.13).
Sing songs that emphasize the initial letter in children's names (see *More Than Singing,* activity 7.13).

6.10 Letter-Bead Twist
Literacy Manipulative

Description

This teacher-made manipulative consists of letter beads or cubes mounted on a dowel. Children can rotate the letter blocks to create a wide variety of words. This material helps children realize the significance of letter placement in words.

Left Block	*Center Block*	*Right Block*
letters s, r, p, c	letters a, i, o, u	letters t, n, d, p

Child's Level

This activity is most appropriate for preschool and kindergarten children.

Materials

- 3 wooden cubes, 1 inch across, with a ¼-inch hole drilled through each
- ³⁄₁₆-inch dowel, 5 inches long, inserted through the cubes
- two small beads glued to the ends of the dowels to keep the cubes from falling off
- press-on letters to mount on the cubes, or dark permanent marker to print the letters

Helpful Hint

Letter beads are available in some craft or fabric stores. Look for beads that have the letters you need for this activity.

What to Look For

Children will rotate the letters and try to determine the words they have created.

Some children will focus on individual letters rather than words.

At first, some children may have trouble understanding that not every combination they come up with makes a word.

Some children will begin to sound out new words phonetically.

Modification

Add word cards to the activity after children have had experience rotating the letters to create new words.

Comments & Questions to Extend Thinking

What letter did you put at the beginning of your word?
Let's turn the middle block to a new letter and see what happens to the word.
Can you make another word with these blocks?

Comments & Questions to Encourage Phonetic Awareness

Listen: The letter "u" makes an "uh" sound in these words.
Let's say the sound of each letter and see if we can figure out what your word says.
What letter do you need on this block to change "cat" to "cap"?

Integrated Curriculum Activities

Put a letter-bead twist in the writing area. Children may wish to copy the words they make.
Change the words to the song "Bingo" to include the words the children make:

> We made a word at school today, and this is
> what it said–oh,
> C-a-t, c-a-t, c-a-t, and *cat* was the word–oh.

6.11 Letter Blocks
Literacy Manipulative

Description
Letter blocks allow children to build words both horizontally and vertically. They are available in several sizes. Pattern cards model words that children can form with the blocks.

Child's Level
This activity is most appropriate for preschool and kindergarten children.

Materials
◆ wooden letter blocks
◆ word cards, created by drawing squares and printing letters inside, to look like the blocks
◆ stickers, to illustrate the word cards
◆ laminating materials, for the word cards

What to Look For
Children will rotate the blocks to look at the letters.
Some children will use the blocks to create words, such as those on the word cards.
Some children will try to spell their names with the blocks.
Some children will build with the blocks.
Some children will line up the blocks and then wonder what they spell.
At first, some children will have difficulty understanding that not every arrangement of letters makes a word.

Helpful Hints
Look for letter blocks in craft stores or toy stores.

You can create your own letter blocks by applying stick-on letters to 1-inch cubes.

Modifications

Start with horizontal word cards for children who are less experienced with written language, since this is the standard way words are printed.

For older or more experienced children, include pattern cards with both vertical and horizontal words.

Comments & Questions to Extend Thinking

What letters do you need to make this word?

If you put the letters this way—t, a, r—they spell "tar" instead of "rat." Where do you have to put the "r" to spell "rat"?

Can you find another letter that looks like this one?

Comments & Questions to Encourage Phonetic Awareness

Ben wants to know what his word says. Let's say the sound of each letter and see if we can figure it out.

What sound does this word start with?

You made the word "car." Put an "e" on the end, and listen to what happens to the word.

Integrated Curriculum Activities

Cut white labels into squares and print letters on them. Children can use the stickers to write words or experiment with letters.

Ask parents to save the letter labels from videotapes. They can be included in the art or writing areas.

Put letter blocks in the block area. Children may use them to spell the names of buildings that they construct.

6.12 Foam Letters
Sensory Table Manipulative

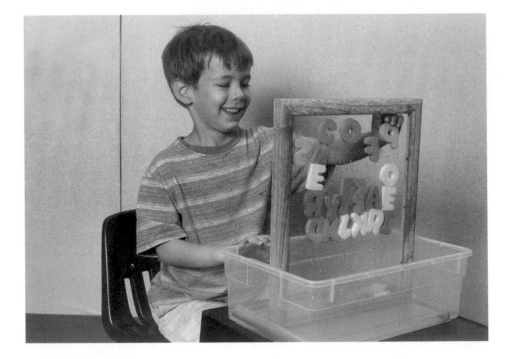

Description
Foam letters stick to Plexiglas surfaces when wet. In this activity, children adhere foam letters to Plexiglas easels in the water table. They can explore letter and word formations tactilely through sensory play. This is an excellent way to extend literacy to other areas of the classroom and encourage literacy development through another medium. Since children can work on both sides of the frames, four children can use the materials at a time.

Child's Level
This activity is most appropriate for preschool or kindergarten children.

Materials
- two Plexiglas easels, made by mounting 14- by 16-inch pieces of Plexiglas in inexpensive wooden frames and screwing two strips of wood to the bottom of each frame so that they stand vertically
- foam letters, available commercially or cut from foam board
- water table or plastic tubs with water

Helpful Hints
To cut the Plexiglas, score it with a mat knife and carefully break it along the line.

Foam board, which comes in a variety of colors, is available in craft stores. It can be cut with scissors or used with an Ellison machine.

Apply shellac to the wood to protect it from the water.

What to Look For

Children will be fascinated with the way the letters stick to the easels.

Children will observe how the letters appear as they look through the Plexiglas at the letters on the other side.

Some children will attempt to write words or their names with the letters.

Some children will sort the letters by type on the easels.

Modification

For older children who have already had the opportunity to explore the properties of the foam letters, mount laminated word cards or name tags near the water table to serve as print models.

Comments & Questions to Extend Thinking

Can you find another letter that looks like this one?

What letters do you need to spell your name?

If you put an "o" next to your "g," it will spell "go."

Comments & Questions to Encourage Phonetic Awareness

I see a row of "s's" on your easel. "S" makes a "ss" sound like "snake."

What sound do you think "o" makes?

Sometimes "o" makes an "ah" sound, like in "hop." Do you want to see how that looks?

Integrated Curriculum Activities

Read *Chicka Chicka Boom Boom,* by Bill Martin Jr. and John Archambault (New York: Simon & Schuster, 1989), to the class. Children may wish to act out the story with the foam letters.

Sing the alphabet song as children play with the letters. Some children may try to assemble the letters in alphabetical order.

Play letter games, such as "Alphabet Bingo" (activity 6.8) or "Grab Bag" (activity 6.5).

6.13 Sponge Letters
Art Manipulative

Description
Sponge letters dipped in paint create interesting impressions on paper. They allow children to experiment with letters through an art medium. Children can rotate the letters and notice the effect, create patterns or free-form designs, or use the letters to spell words. The foam letters can be used at the easel or at a special activity table.

Child's Level
This activity is most appropriate for preschool or kindergarten children.

Materials
- sponge letters
- small dish of paint for each painting station
- white paper, 12 by 18 inches or 18 by 22 inches
- smocks

Helpful Hint
Sponge letters are available commercially. They can also be cut from household sponges. To make sponge letters, trace letters onto the sponges with a permanent marker and cut them out with a mat knife.

What to Look For

Children will experiment by dipping the sponge letters in paint and seeing how they look on the paper.

Children will rotate the letters as they place them on the paper.

Some children will search for the first letters of their names.

Some children will name the letters as they create paint impressions.

Some children will write words with the sponges.

Some children will create letter impressions, but then wipe over all the letters with paint.

Modification

Start with one color of paint so children focus on the shapes of the letters rather than on colors. Later, other colors of paint can be added.

Comments & Questions to Extend Thinking

I see "s's" going in lots of different directions on your paper.

Look: You turned the "m" upside down, and it made a "w."

Can you think of a word that starts with this letter?

Comments & Questions to Encourage Phonetic Awareness

What letter do you need to make the first sound in "Mommy"?

Charlie wants to write "stop." What sounds do you hear in "stop"?

I see a "k" on your paper. It makes a "kuh" sound, like in "Kathy."

Integrated Curriculum Activities

Use letter-shaped cookie cutters with paint. Children can compare the cookie-cutter prints to the sponge prints.

Put letter stamps in the writing center (see chapter 5).

Use letter molds or ice cube trays with playdough or other modeling substances (activity 6.14).

6.14 Letter Molds
Art Manipulative

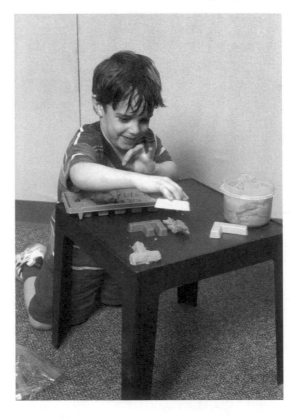

Description
Letter molds enable children to physically explore the form and shape of letters. They encourage children to examine letters tactilely as well as visually. As children conform playdough or moist sand to the boundaries of the molds, they gain an improved sense of the lines and curves that combine to form individual letters. When children remove the modeling substance from the molds, they can rotate the letter images and observe how they look in various positions. This helps children identify letters in the many forms that they take in our daily lives.

Child's Level
This activity is appropriate for preschool or kindergarten children.

Materials
- large, plastic letter molds, letter cookie cutters, or alphabet ice cube trays
- modeling substance, such as playdough or moist sand

Helpful Hint
If you use sand with the molds, be sure it is moist so it will hold its form.

What to Look For

Children will explore the letter boundaries of the molds by attempting to fill them with the modeling substance.

Children will remove the modeling material from the molds to see how the letters look.

Some children will trace, rotate, and reform the letters with their fingers.

Some children will name the letters.

Some children will use the molded letters to spell words or their names.

Modification

Start with larger, individual letter molds for younger or less experienced children. Switch to smaller molds of the complete alphabet for older children.

Comments & Questions to Extend Thinking

I see a circle and a straight line in this letter "p" that you made.

What would you have to do to your "o" to turn it into a "q"?

Turn your letter "m" around and see what happens. Look: It's a "w" now.

Comments & Questions to Encourage Phonetic Awareness

Paul made a "p" with the playdough. It makes a "puh" sound, like the beginning of his name.

I want to make "go" with my letter molds. What letter makes the "guh" sound?

"A" makes the beginning sound for "Amy" and for "Anne."

Integrated Curriculum Activities

Include letter molds in the sand table.

Use individual letter molds with paint as printing tools.

Compare the impressions made by sponge letters dipped in paint to those made by letter cookie cutters.

Use the letter molds with snow in the winter.

6.15 Letter Stencils
Writing Area Manipulative

Description
Letter stencils provide a bridge for children who are transitioning into writing. They help children both feel and see the combination of curved and straight lines that make up individual letters. Like other materials, the stencils should be available for children when they are interested and not used for drill or practice. The stencils can be placed in the art or writing areas for easy access by the children.

Child's Level
This activity is most appropriate for older preschool or kindergarten children.

Look for letter stencils in office-supply stores or school-supply sections of department stores.

Be sure the pencils are kept sharpened so they will fit inside the stencils.

Materials
- several plastic letter stencils, with standard print
- regular or colored pencils

What to Look For
Children will draw inside the boundaries of the stencils and look at the results.

Some children will be very excited to see that they have produced a letter.

Some children will try to write the entire alphabet.

Some children will attempt to write their names or other words with the stencils once they become adept at positioning the stencils on their paper.

Modification

Tape the stencils to the paper for children who have trouble
holding the stencil steady while writing. The tape can be
discontinued as children become more experienced and
adept at holding the stencil with one hand while writing
with the other.

Comments & Questions to Extend Thinking

Draw inside the holes on this stencil and see what your lines
make.

Can you find an "A" on your stencil? Look: It's the first letter.

What letter is last on your stencil?

Your "k" is all straight lines, but your "b" has straight and curved
lines.

Comments & Questions to Encourage Phonetic Awareness

Tammy made a "t" for the "tuh" sound at the beginning of
her name.

Ivan wants to write "zoo." What letter does he need first?

Two "o's" go together to make the next sound in "zoo." Can you
think of another word that has that sound? (Answers might
include moon, room, soon, and so on.)

Integrated Curriculum Activities

Sing the alphabet song along with children who are interested as
they write.

Use alphabet pasta as a collage material in the art area.

Include letter puzzles in the manipulative area.

Description

This activity includes flannelboard versions of the images from the classic children's book *It Looked Like Spilt Milk*, by Charles G. Shaw (New York: Harper, 1947). Children quickly learn the words to this predictable text. They can act out the story with the flannel pieces as they reread the book.

Child's Level

This activity is appropriate for preschool or kindergarten children.

Materials

- flannelboard, made by adhering dark blue felt, 9 by 12 inches, to heavy cardboard
- silhouettes of the images from the book, cut from white felt
- word cards (optional)
- copy of the book

Helpful Hint

Tape the edges of the flannel board with blue plastic tape for a nicer finish.

What to Look For

Children will quickly remember the repeating text of the book and
will be able to retell the story.

Children will add pieces to the flannelboard to correlate with the
sequence of the book.

Some children will match word cards to the felt shapes.

Modification

For older or more experienced children, include word cards
to correspond to the felt pieces. The cards can be laminated
and attached to the flannelboard with a hooked fabric such
as Velcro.

Comments & Questions to Extend Thinking

Sometimes it looked like a . . . . (Pause, so the child can insert the
appropriate word.)

What do you think this word says? (Point to the word in the book
that matches the image in the illustration, such as "tree.")

Comments & Questions to Encourage Phonetic Awareness

Brittany says it looked like a tree. What sounds do you hear in
"tree"?

Let's find the word "tree" on this page and see what letters it has.

Integrated Curriculum Activities

Sing songs about clouds (see *More Than Singing*, activity 2.8).

Read other books about clouds and weather, such as *The Wind
Blew*, by Pat Hutchins (New York: Macmillan, 1974), and *The
Cloud Book*, by Tomie de Paola (New York: Scholastic, 1975).

Put white pom-poms in blue water in the sensory table. Children
can fish them out with tongs.

Make cloud pictures by putting white paint on blue paper and let-
ting the children blow the paint with straws (see *More Than
Painting*, activity 5.13).

Use cloud stickers on blue poster board to create cloud grid
boards for math games. (See *More Than Counting*, chapter 4,
for information about grid games.)

6.17 Fish Hunt
Story Extension

Description
Children love the predictable book *Blue Sea,* by Robert Kalan (New York: Greenwillow, 1979). A succession of increasingly large fish chase and attempt to eat one another. This activity includes colorful fish cut from foam board to correspond to the characters in the book. Children can place the fish on Plexiglas easels in the water table as they recreate the story.

Helpful Hint
Details can be drawn on the fish with permanent markers.

Child's Level
This activity is most appropriate for preschool or kindergarten children.

Materials
- fish in various sizes and colors, cut from foam board, to correspond to the characters in the book
- 2 Plexiglas easels (see activity 6.12 for directions)
- copy of the book
- laminated word cards, with the words "little fish," "big fish," "bigger fish," "biggest fish," and "ouch" printed on them, to mount next to the sensory table (optional)

What to Look For
Children will listen with great anticipation to the story.
Children will use the foam-board pieces to retell the story.
Some children will match the word cards to the appropriate fish.
Some children will compare the word cards to the corresponding words in the book.
Children will enjoy pointing to the word "ouch" as the fish get caught.

Modification
Older children may wish to create their own fish to add to the story. They can draw their fish on foam board and cut them out.

Comments & Questions to Extend Thinking
Which fish comes after "big fish"?
Is there a fish that's larger than "bigger fish"?
What happened to "biggest fish"?

Comments & Questions to Encourage Phonetic Awareness
Listen to the sound the "o" and "u" make in "ouch."
Are these words the same? (Compare the word cards for "big" and "bigger.")
Listen to the sound the "e-r" makes at the end of "bigger."

Integrated Curriculum Activities
Sing songs about fish (see *More Than Singing*, activity 2.15).
Put blank books shaped like fish in the writing center along with word cards of sea animals.
Add a beach to the dramatic play area. Use a small, plastic wading pool filled with sand for the beach.
Read other sea books, such as *Tough Boris*, by Mem Fox (New York: Harcourt, 1994), and *Swimmy*, by Leo Lionni (New York: Knopf, 1963).

6.18 Baby Owls
Story Extension

Description

Since young children are often still dealing with fears about separation, the popular children's book *Owl Babies,* by Martin Waddell (Cambridge, MA: Candlewick, 1992), is very appealing. In this activity, children use owl puppets to reenact the story. Taking an active role in the book sharing helps children remain focused on the story and better understand the characters and the story elements, such as the feelings of the baby owls.

Child's Level

This activity is most appropriate for preschool or kindergarten children.

Materials

- ◆ 3 small baby-owl puppets or toys
- ◆ 1 adult-owl puppet or toy
- ◆ copy of the book

What to Look For

Children will use the puppets to play the roles of the characters in the book.
Many children will identify with the feelings of the baby owls.
Children will repeat the predictable phrases from the book.
Children will ask to hear the book read many times.

Modification

Older children may wish to create their own owl puppets to use with the book by drawing owls on paper, cutting them out, and mounting the owls on sticks.

Comments & Questions to Extend Thinking

What do you think Bill said?

Why do you think all of the baby owls wanted to sit on the branch together?

Comments & Questions to Encourage Phonetic Awareness

What sound does "Percy" start with?

Listen to the word "Mommy." It has two "m" sounds in it.

Integrated Curriculum Activities

Put word cards with the names of the baby owls in the writing area.

Create math games with an owl theme (see *Much More than Counting,* activities 6.2, 7.2a, and 7.2b).

Put bird nests in the science area for children to examine (see *More Than Magnets,* activity 2.8).

Read other books about owls, such as *Good-Night Owl,* by Pat Hutchins (New York: Macmillan, 1972), and *Owl: See How They Grow,* by Mary Ling (New York: Dorling Kindersley, 1992).

 **The Mitten**

Story Extension

Description

Children are fascinated with the traditional Ukrainian story "The Mitten," in which a series of normally incompatible animals share space inside a child's lost mitten. Several book versions are available, including *The Mitten,* by Jan Brett (New York: Putnam, 1989). This activity provides children with the necessary props to reenact the story: a mitten and small plastic animals to correspond to the animals in the book.

Child's Level

This activity is most appropriate for preschool or kindergarten children.

Materials

◆ adult-size white mitten
◆ small plastic animals: mole, rabbit, hedgehog, owl, badger, fox, bear, and mouse
◆ copy of the book
◆ tray or basket, to contain all the pieces

What to Look For

Children will use the toy animals to act out the sequence of the story.

Some children will remember the sequence of the appearance of the characters.

Children will ask to hear the book read many times.

Children will participate in telling the story.

 *Helpful Hint*

Science or nature stores often have bins of toy animals, including some of the more unusual animals found in the story.

Modification
The board-book version of Jan Brett's *The Mitten* has less text than
the original version. It can be used with younger children.

Comments & Questions to Extend Thinking
What animal found the mitten first?

How do you think the animals felt when the fox tried to get in?

Do you think the bear can fit in the mitten?

Find the hedgehog. It needs to go into the mitten next.

Comments & Questions to Encourage Phonetic Awareness
What sound do you hear at the end of "fox."

The name of the letter "x" and the sound it makes are almost
the same.

"Mole," "mouse," and "mitten" all start with the same sound.

Integrated Curriculum Activities
Use a sheet to create a giant mitten. Children can play the roles
of the animals and dramatize the story.

Create a gross-motor math game to correspond to *The Mitten*.
Children can roll a large die and hop along a path to the mitten
(see *Much More Than Counting*, activity 1.15).

Put collage materials that resemble snow in the art area. Cotton
balls, pieces of white tissue paper, white and silver glitter, and
paper confetti are possibilities (see *More Than Painting*,
activity 2.7).

Incorporate the word for snow in various languages into a song
(see *More Than Singing*, activity 2.6).

CHAPTER 7

Environmental Print

Several children played in the dramatic play area, which was set up like a post office. A dispute erupted, and the teacher approached the area. All the children wanted to pretend to sell stamps behind the counter. The teacher directed the children's attention to a sign above the individual mailboxes and read, "You can mail your letters here." One of the children immediately declared herself the mail carrier instead of a clerk in the post office. The other children anxiously awaited her delivery of mail to their mailboxes.

▲ ▲ ▲

Casey and Alexander sat at the science center, which contained a display of pinwheels. The two children began to bang the pinwheels on the table instead of experimenting with how to make them move. The teacher approached and read the sign posted behind the display. The sign read, How many pinwheels can you move using the bellows? *Casey and Alexander changed their focus to using the bellows to move all the pinwheels at the same time.*

▲ ▲ ▲

Meaningful, functional, and interesting print is part of the environment surrounding all young children. Children often recognize the logo for their favorite fast food restaurant, toothpaste, or juice. They see adults copy recipes from magazines or telephone numbers from the telephone book. Likewise, the early childhood classroom contains an abundance of environmental print. Signs in the classroom tell children whether an area is open or closed. Labels on the art shelves help children organize the materials. Recipe cards provide the necessary information to make biscuits. Message boards and other relevant messages encourage children to write in response to the environmental print.

Teachers' Questions

What is meant by environmental print?

Environmental print includes traditional signs, such as exit, stop, *or* detour, *and labels on food packages. It also includes teacher-made environmental-print activities for the classroom.* Teachers can optimize children's interest in print by highlighting traditional print in the environment and by designing activities to include meaningful and functional print in the classroom. For example, teachers might comment on the print that children observe during field trips or when children express an interest in signs in the school environment. Teachers may also design relevant environmental print to include in the classroom.

What kinds of environmental-print activities can teachers design for the classroom?

Teachers can design relevant labels, signs, charts, and writing-response activities to include throughout the classroom. The first words children usually learn to read are their names. Therefore, teachers should include the children's names in a variety of places in the classroom (activities 7.2 and 7.3). Teachers can also include other labels and signs to give information or help organize the environment. For example, teachers might place a *Closed* sign in certain curriculum areas during the transition to group time or lunch. They might label shelves in a dramatic play area set up as a grocery store to help children return the cans, produce, and frozen foods to the appropriate location. Teachers can also include relevant print in dramatic play, block, and art areas. Activities 7.6 through 7.8 give suggestions for ways teachers can include print in those areas.

Charts, such as those used to take attendance or identify jobs, can also be included in the classroom on a regular basis. Teachers may want to redesign these charts throughout the year to keep children interested in them. Activities 7.2, 7.3, and 7.4 are examples. Other types of charts, such as recipe charts and menus, may also be used throughout the year.

Teachers should also plan environmental-print activities that encourage children to write in response to the print. For example, waiting lists and message boards allow children to write their names, make requests, or give information to others.

Books can enhance the learning materials in many curriculum areas and help to integrate print throughout the environment. For example, if a class is interested in insects, the teacher might include a book about insects along with insect models in the science area. In the block area, the teacher might introduce a book about a variety of types of homes. Books and magazines can also be incorporated into the dramatic play area. For example, baby board books might be included in a dramatic play area designed as a nursery, while magazines might be incorporated into a doctor area.

Why are environmental-print activities important in the early childhood classroom?

Environmental-print activities provide opportunities for children to construct important concepts about reading. Charts, labels, signs, message boards, and other activities in the environment help children construct the knowledge that print communicates information and that the meaning of print can be functional. For example, the job chart helps children know when they have a specific responsibility, the sign in dramatic play identifies the area as a pizza parlor, and the labels on the art shelf help children know where to return the materials. More information about how children learn to read can be found in chapter 1.

Some environmental-print activities provide opportunities for children to construct important concepts about writing. Message boards, lunch notes, and waiting lists help children understand the role of the writer as well as the role of the reader. They learn that they can record their thoughts and ideas for others to read. They also learn specific mechanics of writing, such as letter formation and the necessity for a particular sequence of letters to form specific words. In addition, children gradually refine their writing attempts and progress through the developmental stages of writing. More information about writing can be found in chapters 1 and 4.

What should teachers consider when including environmental print in the classroom?

Teachers should consider
- *the interests of the children*
- *the content of the print*
- *the relevance of the print to other curricular activities*
- *the clarity of the printing*

Children are much more likely to attend to environmental print when it relates to something of interest to them. For example, children interested in a grocery store in the dramatic play area will often look closely at the food labels, while children who are interested in building roads in the block area may attend to small road signs included in the area.

The content of the environmental print should be meaningful to the children. While they may ignore labels that aren't particularly important to them, such as a word card that says *chair* on the back of a chair, they often attend carefully to more important messages, such as one that says the faucet is broken at the sink.

When environmental print relates to other items of high interest in the curriculum, such as labels for toy zoo animals in the dramatic play area following a trip to the zoo, children pay particular attention to it. In all cases, print that is included in the classroom should be clearly formed, with adequate space between the letters and the words for children to distinguish them.

What should teachers avoid when planning environmental-print activities for the classroom?

Teachers should avoid overwhelming the classroom with environmental print. Children are unable to focus on the purpose of print when it is everywhere in the room or the print is not meaningful to them. For example, if a classroom is decorated with number and alphabet charts hung high on the walls and each curriculum area is labeled, children quickly lose interest in the print. The charts on the walls are too high for children to look at, and they can easily identify the areas of the classroom without the label. On the other hand, children may be very interested in a new sign in the music area that encourages them to think about a response to the question, *Which of these triangles sound the same?* They often pay close attention to a sign on the fish tank that reads either, *Please feed the fish* or *The fish have been fed.*

While children rarely show sustained interest in labels on the wall, chair, and table, they may be very interested in labels for their names and the name of the class pet. Functional labels for the various art materials are useful and helpful in organizing an area for children. Likewise, children are very interested in the labels on the shelves in the dramatic play area when it is set up as a bakery. They quickly find the labels for the cookies, pretzels, and muffins when it is clean-up time.

How can teachers encourage phonetic awareness through environmental print?

Teachers can take advantage of opportunities throughout the day to highlight phonetic concepts within the context of the environmental print. Children often ask for assistance reading signs, labels, charts, and other environmental print in the classroom. Teachers can point out phonetic concepts, relate the print to what children already know about letters and sounds, and ask questions to help children create letter–symbol relationships. Each activity in this chapter includes suggestions for specific comments and questions to encourage phonetic awareness.

How can teachers assess children's literacy development through environmental print?

Teachers can observe children during their independent use of environmental-print activities in the classroom and save samples of children's written responses. Teachers can record their observations on index cards collected for each child or in a notebook for each child. Some teachers keep these anecdotal records and writing samples as part of each child's portfolio along with other information and artifacts. Some teachers may use checklists to document the child's progress in literacy development. A sample reading assessment form is included in appendix C, and a sample writing assessment form is included in appendix D.

Environmental-Print Activities

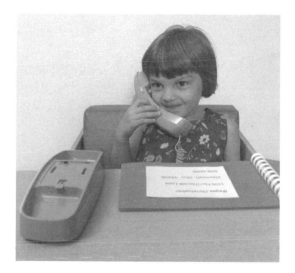

7.1 Classroom Routines
Name Cards

Description

The first words children learn to read are their names and the names of other children. This activity shows teachers a variety of ways to utilize name cards throughout the classroom, from lunch tags and cubby markers to group-time place cards. Teachers should use a watercolor marker and standard alphabet model to print the name of each child and teacher in the class. The letters should be uniform in size and with sufficient spacing between letters to allow children to distinguish one letter from another.

Child's Level

These activities are most appropriate for preschool and kindergarten children.

Materials

- ◆ sentence strips, cut into 8-inch sections, for group-time or cubby name cards
- ◆ tag board or poster board, or 3-by-5-inch index cards, for lunch or snack name cards
- ◆ clear plastic picture frames, for holding lunch or snack cards, one per child
- ◆ laminating film or clear self-adhesive plastic, for covering name cards

◆ small baskets, for holding name cards throughout the class-room, such as in the block or art areas

What to Look For
Children will read their names and the names of other children and teachers in a variety of places in the classroom.
Some children will copy the name cards.
Some children will read their names by looking at the first letter alone.
Children will compare letters on the various name cards.
Children will locate their personal spaces or their lunch or snack seats by recognizing their names.
Some children will use the name cards placed at the writing center as a model for writing their names in the art, easel, or other areas of the classroom.

Modification
Kindergarten children may be very interested in name cards that include both their first and last names.

Comments & Questions to Extend Thinking
You can use your name card to write your name on your art paper.
Look for your name at the lunch table. Who is sitting with you today?
Will you set up the mats for group time? Nitara wants to sit next to Amy.

Comments & Questions to Encourage Phonemic Awareness
Your name begins with a "c" just like Carl's, but the last letter of your name is "y." The last letter of "Carl" is an "l." Can you hear the difference? Look for a name that begins with "c" and ends with "y" to find your name.
Two children in this class have names that begin with the same sound as "Brenda." Do you know who they are?
Look: Mary's name starts with an "m." It makes a "muh" sound. What's another word that starts with that sound?

Integrated Curriculum Activities
Plan interactive charts that utilize the children's names (activities 3.1, 3.2, and 3.3).
Use the name cards from the writing center to transition children from group time to the next activity.

Helpful Hint

Commercial blank name cards with decorated borders are available through school-supply catalogs.

7.2 Clouds
Attendance Chart

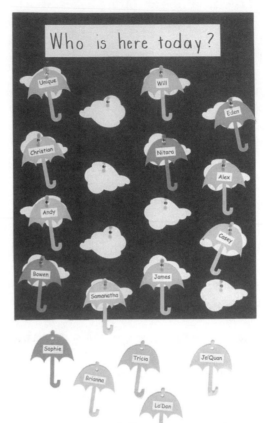

Description

A good way to encourage emergent reading is to allow children to take attendance by putting a fancy name card on an attendance chart. The chart can be made using notepaper or shape cutouts to coordinate with seasonal changes or high-interest curriculum activities. The example shown is made with cloud cutouts. The name cards are umbrella shapes made from yellow construction paper, printed with each child's name, and laminated for durability.

Child's Level

This activity is most appropriate for preschool children or kindergarten children at the beginning of the year.

Materials

- ◆ blue poster board
- ◆ white sentence strip, for printing *Who is here today?*
- ◆ white cloud-shaped paper (enough for each child in the class)

- umbrella cutouts for each child's name card (punch a hole in each umbrella, which allows it to hang on the paper fastener)
- ¾-inch paper fastener, for each cloud shape
- lamination film, for the individual umbrella name cards and for the chart

What to Look For

Initially, some very young children will put any name on the chart.

Some children will select their name card by looking at the first letter alone.

Some children will be able to select their name card from a small number of name cards.

Some children will be able to select their name card from the large number of name cards.

Children will compare names that start with the same letter.

Children will read the name cards of other children.

Modifications

Children can make the name cards by painting white umbrella cutouts with pastel watercolors. Later, the teacher can write the children's names on the cutouts and laminate them.

Substitute balloon, bird, or other appropriate cutouts for the name cards.

Comments & Questions to Extend Thinking

Who is here today? Look on the attendance chart to find out.

How many children are here today? How can we find out?

Are these children here yet—Rachel, Anne, and Jesse? You can look at the attendance chart to find out.

Let's find all the names that start with "j."

Comments & Questions to Encourage Phonetic Awareness

Jason's name begins with a "juh" sound just like Jacqueline's name.

Whose name begins with the same sound as Ayanna? Do they both begin with the same letter?

Shannon, you chose Shawn's name for the chart. His name has some of the same letters as yours, but "Shannon" has two "n's" in the middle and "Shawn" doesn't.

Integrated Curriculum Activities

Sing songs about clouds and rain (see *More Than Singing*, activities 2.8, 2.10, and 4.13).

Read books about clouds, such as *It Looked Like Spilt Milk*, by Charles G. Shaw (New York: Harper, 1947), and *The Cloud Book*, by Tomie de Paola (New York, Scholastic, 1975).

Helpful Hints

Use a thumbtack to start a hole in the chart before inserting the paper fastener.

Be sure to cut the holes in the umbrellas large enough to slip over the paper fastener easily.

7.3 Leaf Attendance Chart and Gross-Motor-Room Chart

Description

In some settings, children may choose to participate in activities in more than one room. Teachers will want to monitor both the location of children and the numbers of children in each room. In this activity, the leaf attendance chart and the gross-motor-room chart allow children to move their name card from one chart to the other as they select activities in the different rooms. Children who want to be with a friend must carefully read the name cards to locate the friend.

Child's Level

This activity is most appropriate for preschool and kindergarten children.

Helpful Hint

Use very small pieces of Velcro on the leaf name cards to make it easier for children to remove them from the chart. Laminate the chart before attaching the Velcro to each leaf on the chart.

Materials

- white poster board
- white sentence strips, for printing *Who is here today?* and *Who is in the gross-motor room?*
- green construction paper, for mounting the sentence strips before gluing them to the poster board
- leaf shapes, cut from green construction paper (enough for each child in the class plus the number of spaces available in the gross-motor room)
- yellow leaf cutouts, for each child's name card
- self-adhesive Velcro-brand fastener
- laminating film, for attaching the leaf name cards to the chart

What to Look For

Initially, some very young children will put any name on the chart.

Some children will select the name card by looking at the first letter alone.

Some children will be able to select their name card from a small number of names.

Some children will be able to select their name card from a large number of names.

Children will look to see who is in the gross-motor room.

Some children will look for a friend's name so they can place their name card next to it.

Modifications

For kindergarten children, both first and last names can be printed on the name cards.

Use light green construction paper for leaf name cards in spring.

Use red, yellow, orange, and brown construction paper for leaf name cards in autumn.

Comments & Questions to Extend Thinking

Who is in the gross-motor room now? Can you find their names on the chart?

How many children have not come to school yet? See if you can read their name cards.

Whose name is next to yours?

Help me read who is in the gross-motor room.

Comments & Questions to Encourage Phonetic Awareness

I can hear the sound for the letter "o" in the words "gross" and "motor." What other sounds can you hear in those words?

Look at the beginning of "who." What sound do you hear? Sometimes "w" and "h" go together to make an "h" sound.

Integrated Curriculum Activities

Plan an autumn writing center in the classroom (activities 5.2 and 5.3).

Plan a printing activity using leaf-shaped cookie cutters (see *More Than Painting*, activity 5.17).

Create a big book based on an autumn poem (activity 2.2).

Description

In many early childhood classrooms, children take turns feeding the fish, watering the plants, and performing other jobs. They are eager to know when it is their turn to have a job. This chart uses photographs or simple illustrations to help children read the list of jobs. It also encourages them to learn to read the names of the children in the class. The teacher places the appropriate name cards on the job chart each day. In this example, children do not interact with the name cards as they do in activities 7.2 and 7.3.

Child's Level

This chart is most appropriate for preschool and kindergarten children.

Materials

- ◆ poster board
- ◆ sentence strip, for printing, "Do you have a job today?"
- ◆ photographs or simple illustrations, to represent various classroom jobs
- ◆ 3-by-5-inch index cards, printed with each child's name and laminated
- ◆ clear laminating film, to make pockets for the name cards

What to Look For

Children will eagerly look for their names on the job chart.
Some children will announce the names of children who have a job each day.
Some children will identify the names by the first letter only.

Helpful Hint

Computer clip art may be a resource for simple illustrations for the chart.

Modifications

Post a weekly schedule for the jobs. This helps children anticipate when they will have a job and makes waiting for a turn more tolerable.

Eliminate the picture cues for older groups of children. Many older children will be able to read the chart.

Comments & Questions to Extend Thinking

Do you have a job today? Let's look at the job chart to find out.

Who is going to feed the fish today? How can you find out?

How many more days until you have a job?

James, Katy says you have a job today. Go see what it is.

Comments & Questions to Encourage Phonetic Awareness

Tomorrow it is Isaac's turn to set up the mats for group. What letter should I look for at the beginning of his name?

Julie and Jessica both have a job today. How do you know which name card is Julie's and which name card is Jessica's?

Integrated Curriculum Activities

At group time, sing a song that includes the children's names and the jobs they had.

Talk with the children about jobs they may have at home.

7.5 Open or Closed?

Description

Signs that convey meaning are important and are readily
remembered by children. Many teachers close certain areas of
the classroom at the end of the day or during a major transition,
such as before lunch or naptime. In this example, the teacher
makes a sign for the dramatic play area, *The doctor's office is
open.* The word *open* is printed in a different color of marker to
draw attention to it. A separate *closed* card, also written in a
different color of marker, is available to use with the sign.
When the area is not open, children can alter the meaning of the
sentence by placing the *closed* card on the sign. Children eagerly
read the sign to find out whether the area is open or closed. As
children become familiar with the letters and sounds in the
words *open* and *closed,* they often use that information to help
them read or spell other high-interest words.

Child's Level

This activity is appropriate for preschool, kindergarten, and
first-grade children. Older children may want to make the sign
themselves.

Materials

◆ white or colored sentence strip, for printing the sign
◆ white or colored poster board, for mounting the sign

- white or colored sentence strip, for making the *closed* word card (the word card should be a size that completely covers the word *open)*
- ¾-inch paper fastener
- lamination or clear contact paper, for covering the sign

What to Look For

Some children will ask to open or close the area by changing the word card.

Some children will read the sign and tell others whether the area is open or closed.

A few children may show their parents the sign and read it to them.

Some children may want to copy the word *closed* for use in another area of the classroom.

Modifications

For younger or less experienced children, begin with separate *open* and *closed* signs to introduce the concept.

Use the same sentence format for other dramatic play areas, such as grocery store, restaurant, and laundry.

Comments & Questions to Extend Thinking

How do you know if the doctor's office is open or closed?

Would you like to open the doctor's office? You can read the sign to the other children.

Comments & Questions to Encourage Phonetic Awareness

What sound do you hear at the beginning of the word "open?"

Look at the word "closed." The first two letters "c" and "l" together make the sound "cluh."

Integrated Curriculum Activities

Set up the dramatic play area as a doctor's office, with white shirts, stethoscopes, a scale, and dolls.

Include relevant books in the reading area, such as *Betsy and the Doctor*, by Gunilla Wolde (New York: Random House, 1978), and *My Doctor*, by Harlow Rockwell (New York: Macmillan, 1973).

Ask the staff of a local emergency medical station to visit the classroom and show children equipment from the emergency vehicle.

Helpful Hint

The teacher should ask children to open or close the area. This will draw attention to the sign.

7.6 Woodworking Guidelines

Wear goggles when using the tools.

Description

Sometimes teachers make print more meaningful and show its power by using it to set classroom guidelines. In this activity, the sign gives children a direction about the use of the workbench: *Wear goggles when using the tools.* Since it is important for children to wear safety goggles, the teacher reinforces the guideline in print. In this example, a picture of a child wearing goggles helps provide a context cue to help children read the print. They are delighted to read the message to each other!

Child's Level

This activity is most appropriate for preschool and kindergarten children.

Materials

- ◆ white or colored sentence strip, for printing the guideline
- ◆ photograph or illustration of a child wearing goggles
- ◆ lamination film or clear contact paper, for covering the sentence strip

What to Look For

Children will comment on the letters and words in the sentence. Some children will notice letters of their name in the sentence. Some children will ask the teacher to read the sentence.

Helpful Hint

School-supply catalogs often show children wearing goggles in advertisements for tools and workbenches. These illustration can be used on signs.

Children will follow the guideline to wear the goggles.
Some children will read the guideline to other children or adults.

Modifications
For older or more experienced children, the picture cue can
  be eliminated from the message.
The sign can also be made using a computer to print the
  guideline.

Comments & Questions to Extend Thinking
The sign says you must wear the goggles to use the woodworking
  bench. You can read the sign to other children if they want to
  use the woodworking bench too.
What do you think these words say?

Comments & Questions to Encourage Phonetic Awareness
Look at all the "g's" in the word "goggles." The "g" makes a "guh"
  sound. Can you hear that sound at the beginning and in the
  middle of the word "goggles?"

Integrated Curriculum Activities
Set up the dramatic play area as a construction site, with flannel
  shirts, hard hats, pretend tools, and goggles.
Plan an activity using golf tees to hammer into Styrofoam and
  include goggles for children to wear (see *More Than Magnets*,
  activity 3.8).
Plan woodworking activities, such as hammering, sawing, and
  drilling.
Create a writing center based on the topic of construction
  (activity 5.9).

7.7 Organizing an Art Area
Signs and Labels

Description
Teachers can use meaningful labels for materials on the art shelves to help organize the area. The labels encourage children to return the materials to the shelves in an orderly fashion. Many materials such as paper, markers, crayons, scissors, glue, tape, and staplers are a permanent part of the art area and remain on the shelves the entire year. The names for these more permanent materials are some of the most appropriate choices for labels in this area. Collage materials, such as ribbon, fabric, and feathers, may change every two to three weeks and do not necessarily need labels.

Child's Level
This activity is most appropriate for preschool and kindergarten children.

Materials
- 3-by-5-inch index cards, or sentence strips, for making the labels
- illustrations of each art material, for the labels
- lamination film or clear self-adhesive paper, to cover the labels
- double-sided tape, to secure the labels to the shelves

Helpful Hint
School-supply catalogs are a good resource for illustrations for the labels.

What to Look For
Children will use the labels to return art materials to the shelves.
Some children will incorrectly read words on the labels as the
name of a child when the first letter is the same, such as *marker*
and *Mary.*
Children will notice a new label and make comments about the
letters or word.

Modifications
For kindergarten children, the labels may be made without the
picture cue.
The labels can be attached to the shelves using a piece of clear
self-adhesive covering such as Con-Tact.

Comments & Questions to Extend Thinking
Where do the staplers go on the art shelves? Look for the label.
How do you know where to return the crayons?

Comments & Questions to Encourage Phonetic Awareness
Listen while I read the words "markers," "crayons," and "scissors."
What sound do you hear at the end of each of the words?
I have to make a label for the tape. Help me decide how to spell
"tape."
I want to return the scissors to the art area. What letter should I
look for to find the word "scissors"?

Integrated Curriculum Activities
Include labels in the dramatic play area when appropriate.
Ask the children what labels may be helpful in other areas of the
classroom.
Take a field trip to a grocery store. Look for aisle and shelf labels.

7.8 Block Area Extension

Description
Teachers sometimes introduce meaningful print into the classroom to encourage children to use materials in a new or different way. In this activity, the teacher adds relevant print and illustrations to the block area. The sentence, "You can build a house for the people," suggests a different way of thinking about the blocks with furniture and accessories. The message can be printed by the teacher or generated on a computer. Illustrations of different types of houses help children predict the meaning of the print. The teacher can vary the suggestion based on observations of children in the area.

Child's Level
This activity is most appropriate for preschool and kindergarten children.

Materials
- sentence strip, for printing the suggestion
- illustrations of different types of houses, to display in the area
- lamination or clear self-adhesive paper, for covering the sentence and illustrations

What to Look For
Children will notice the message and ask someone to read it.
Children will follow the suggestion on the message and build houses in the block area.

Helpful Hints

Take photographs of different types of homes. These can be enlarged on a color copier to display in the block area.

Be sure to include homes and dwellings from various cultures. Parents are a good resource for such pictures.

Some children may read the message to other children.
Some children will comment on the letters and words on the
message.

Modifications
Make signs for other areas of the classroom to stimulate further
thinking. Examples are *Which triangle makes the highest sound?*
(music area) and *How can you sort these nuts?* (science area).

Comments & Questions to Extend Thinking
Which blocks will you use to make the roof of your house?
How many blocks will you need to make another house just like
this one?
Divide the cylinder blocks so each person has the same amount.
Help me read this sign.

Comments & Questions to Encourage Phonetic Awareness
I only hear one sound in "you," but it takes three letters to
write it!
Let's look for the word "house." It starts with a "huh" sound.
What letter do you think makes that sound?

Integrated Curriculum Activities
Plan a construction site in the dramatic play area, with flannel
shirts, hard hats, pretend tools, and tape measures.
Read construction books, such as *Bam Bam Bam,* by Eve Merriam
(New York: Scholastic, 1994), and *Skyscraper Going Up,* by Vicki
Cobb (New York: Crowell, 1987).
Put small colored blocks in the block area as additional props for
building houses.

7.9 Pizza Menu

Description
Many children are familiar with menus in traditional and fast food restaurants. Typically, a menu is either delivered to the table or posted on a sign in the restaurant or drive-through area. This activity suggests one way to include a traditional menu in a dramatic play area set up as a pizza restaurant. After the menu has been laminated, prices can be printed on top of the lamination with a permanent marker. This allows the teacher to change the prices to suit the developmental needs of the children in the group.

Child's Level
This activity is most appropriate for preschool and kindergarten children.

Materials
- yellow poster board or construction paper, 8½ by 11 inches (at least two pieces)
- illustrations or drawings of pizza toppings, milk, and lemonade
- computer or hand-printed labels, for menu—pizza toppings, cheese, tomatoes, pepperoni, green pepper, milk, and lemonade (enough for each menu)
- colored pencils, to decorate the illustrations
- lamination film, for covering the menu

What to Look For

Children will read or point to the items on the menu as they pretend to order food in the restaurant.

Children will misread the words for some of the food items as the name of a child that starts with the same letter. For example, "cheese" may be read as "Charles."

Some children will recognize words on the menu and compare them to the interactive chart, "Pizza is Yummy" (activity 3.9).

Some children will compare letters and words on the menu.

Some children may copy words on the menu as they pretend to place or take an order.

Modifications

For older or more-experienced children, create a more complex menu by adding more food items, such as bread sticks, salad, and ice cream.

The menu can also be designed to fit on a large sheet of poster board and displayed on the wall in the dramatic play area.

Comments & Questions to Extend Thinking

What do you want to order from the menu?

I want to order cheese for my pizza. Help me find the word "cheese" on the menu.

What are the different toppings for the pizzas? Let's look at the menu to find out.

Comments & Questions to Encourage Phonetic Awareness

Look at all the pizza toppings that have double letters—"mushroom," "cheese," "pepperoni," and "green pepper."

I can't find "tomatoes" on the menu. What letters should I look for?

Integrated Curriculum Activities

Set up the dramatic play area as a pizza restaurant, with aprons, pizza boxes, cash register, and order forms, as well as the menus.

Have children vote for their favorite pizza topping and record the results on a graph (see *More Than Counting*, chapter 6).

Plan a cooking activity for children to make their own pizza.

7.10 Making Applesauce

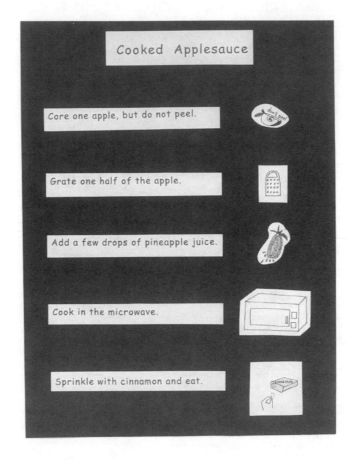

Cooked Applesauce

Core one apple, but do not peel.

Grate one half of the apple.

Add a few drops of pineapple juice.

Cook in the microwave.

Sprinkle with cinnamon and eat.

Description
As children cook, they learn that often a recipe is essential. Posting the directions on a chart allows children to read the recipe along with the teacher and focuses their attention on print. The individual steps are generated on the computer in a font that closely resembles standard manuscript print (Helvetica or Arial) and is at least ¾ inch in height. The directions are glued to the poster board along with illustrations or drawings of the individual ingredients and the tools needed to make applesauce. The picture cues allow children to read the recipe more independently.

Child's Level
This activity is appropriate for preschool, kindergarten, and first-grade children.

Materials
◆ red poster board, 18 by 24 inches

Helpful Hint
If lamination is not available, Con-Tact paper can be used to protect the chart. Be sure to make the chart smaller than the width of the Con-Tact paper.

- individual steps of the recipe, generated on the computer and printed on white paper
- illustrations or drawings of the ingredients and tools needed for the recipe
- colored pencils, for decorating the drawings
- laminating materials, to protect the recipe chart

What to Look For
Children will read the recipe along with the teacher.
Some children will read the words on the chart based on the picture cues.
Children will compare letters and words on the recipe chart.
Some children will be familiar with recipes and talk about their previous experiences.

Modification
Design individual recipe books for this recipe (see activity 7.11).

Comments & Questions to Extend Thinking
What ingredients are needed to make the applesauce?
How many apple slices does each person need for this recipe?
The last step of the recipe says to cook the chopped apples in the microwave.

Comments & Questions to Encourage Phonetic Awareness
The word chop begins with "ch." It makes a "chuh" sound. Listen while I say the word. Can you think of any other words that begin with the "chuh" sound?
Amy's name begins with an "a" and so does the word "apple." Isn't it interesting that the "a" makes a different sound in each word?

Integrated Curriculum Activities
Set up the dramatic play area as a farmer's market, with varieties of produce, including several types of apples.
Plan a field trip to a local grocery store or apple orchard to purchase apples for a cooking activity.
Have children vote for their favorite type of apple and graph the results (see *More Than Counting,* activity 6.5).

7.11 Fruit Salad
Individual Recipe Book

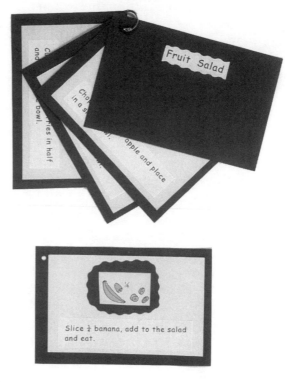

Slice ⅓ banana, add to the salad and eat.

Description

Individual recipe books are another excellent way of focusing children's attention on print while they cook. In this activity, two or three children can independently prepare fruit salad using their own recipe books. One step of the recipe is written on each page of the book. The recipe books give them an opportunity to follow the steps for preparation, while the teacher supervises and assists only when needed.

Helpful Hint

If ribbon is used to hold the pages of the book together, tie it loosely enough for the pages to turn without binding.

Child's Level

This activity is appropriate for older preschool, kindergarten, and first-grade children. Younger children would have difficulty completing the activity without more teacher direction.

Materials

- 5-by-8-inch index cards, for the pages of the recipe book
- illustrations for each step of the recipe
- colored pencils, for decorating the illustrations

- ½-inch plastic comb binding, ½-inch notebook rings, or ribbon, for binding the books
- lamination or clear self-adhesive paper, for covering the pages of the recipe books

What to Look For

Children will read each page of the recipe and follow the directions for making fruit salad.

Some children will need instructions for how to follow the recipe.

A few children will require more assistance in following the recipe but will then complete the activity independently.

Modification

For younger groups of children, the teacher might work with a small group and use only one recipe book rather than individual books.

Comments & Questions to Extend Thinking

Which fruits will we use to make the fruit salad?

How many strawberries will each child need for the recipe?

I like oranges in my fruit salad. Are oranges in this recipe?

Find the recipe card in your book that tells how many grapes to use.

Comments & Questions to Encourage Phonetic Awareness

"Strawberry" begins with same sound as "string." Can you hear the "str" sound in each word?

I want to put a peach in my salad. What sound does "peach" start with?

Listen to the end of "peach." "C" and "h" go together to make that sound.

Integrated Curriculum Activities

Include the book *The Very Hungry Caterpillar*, by Eric Carle (New York: Philomel, 1969), in the reading area.

Set up the dramatic play area as a farmer's market, with aprons, a cash register, and plastic fruits and vegetables.

7.12 Class Phone Book

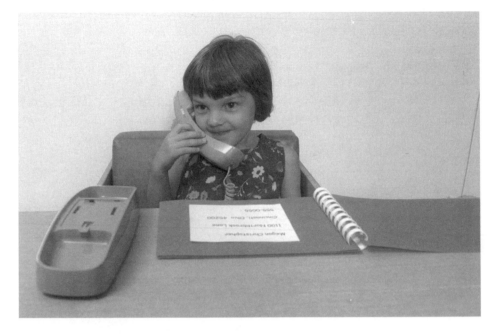

Description
Play telephones are a common accessory in the dramatic play area of many early childhood classrooms. A class telephone book, with each child's name and telephone number, encourages children to look at print as they incorporate the telephone into their play. The telephone book might be a part of the writing center for a first-grade classroom. To create the telephone book, the teacher prints the name and telephone number of each child on paper. The pages can be bound together with a cover labeled *Our Class Telephone Book*.

Child's Level
This activity is most appropriate for older preschool, kindergarten, and first-grade children.

Materials
- plain or lined paper, for printing names and telephone numbers
- construction paper, for the cover
- notebook rings, for binding the pages and cover

What to Look For
Children will look for and read their names and telephone numbers.
Children will look for the names and telephone numbers of their friends.

Helpful Hint

Be sure to ask parents for permission to include their child's telephone number in the class telephone book.

Some children will copy the names and telephone numbers in the book.

Children may begin to remember the order of the alphabet as they search for a specific name in the book.

Some children will begin to distinguish letters from numbers after interacting with the telephone book.

Modifications

An inexpensive address book may also be used to create the class telephone book.

The first and last names of children may be included in the telephone book.

Comments & Questions to Extend Thinking

Who would you like to call on the telephone? Look for her name in the telephone book.

What is your telephone number? Can you find it in the telephone book?

Comments & Questions to Encourage Phonetic Awareness

"Rina" and "Ryan" both begin with the letter "r." What is the next sound you hear in Rina's name? What letter makes that sound?

I want to call Dimitri. What letter should I look for at the beginning of his name?

Integrated Curriculum Activities

Include several telephones in the dramatic play area.

Provide paper and pencils in the dramatic play area. Children may want to copy the names and telephone numbers of their friends (activity 4.18).

7.13 Food Containers

Description

Adding real food containers, such as cake boxes, yogurt contain-ers, and peanut butter jars, is an excellent way to incorporate environmental print into dramatic play. Many children are already familiar with the labels on food. This activity encourages them to further explore print in the environment as they pretend to cook or shop for food. Teachers can also add food containers from a variety of cultures. This introduces children to the writing systems of other peoples. They are often fascinated and excited to see different forms of writing.

Child's Level

This activity is most appropriate for preschool and kindergarten children.

Materials

◆ clean, empty boxes, cans, and plastic food containers, with no sharp edges

What to Look For

Many children will recognize and read some of the food labels.

Some children will misread words on a label as their name.

Children will recognize and compare letters and words on the labels.

Many children will observe differences in the writing on the food containers from other cultures. They may use the illustrations on the labels to read the print.

Modification

Add other household boxes, cans, and plastic containers, such as soap, toothpaste, and laundry detergent, to the dramatic play area.

Comments & Questions to Extend Thinking

What kinds of cereal do you have in the cabinet?

I want to buy some soap and peanut butter. Do you have those in the store?

Comments & Questions to Encourage Phonetic Awareness

"Soup" and "soap" both begin with the letter "s" and end with the letter "p." They both have the same sounds at the beginning and end of the word.

Claire wants to make a cake. Help her write the word "cake." What letter makes the "kuh" sound at the beginning of the word "cake?"

Integrated Curriculum Activities

Set up the dramatic play area as a grocery store. Organize the food boxes and cans into categories, such as frozen foods, canned fruits and vegetables, laundry supplies, and baby supplies.

Read books such as *The Supermarket,* by Anne and Harlow Rockwell (New York: Macmillan, 1979), and *Feast for Ten,* by Cathryn Falwell (New York: Clarion, 1993).

Make math games related to shopping (see *Much More Than Counting,* activities 5.12, 6.10, 7.10a, and 7.10b).

Description

Children are excited when they can "read" print on familiar signs or boxes. Some children like to copy the words. This activity introduces familiar environmental print as a special activity. Children can copy the labels from cans and boxes of food or other household items. The labels should be removed from the cans, and the boxes should be cut apart so they lie flat on the table. This makes it easier for some children to copy the letters.

Child's Level

This activity is most appropriate for older preschool, kindergarten, and first-grade children.

Materials

- various labels and boxes from familiar items, such as cereal, toothpaste, macaroni and cheese, cookies, and peanut butter
- white drawing paper, 8½ by 11 inches
- pencils for each place at the table

What to Look For

Children will copy the largest word or words on the label.
Some children will copy the smallest words, such as the directions, the list of ingredients, and the 800 number for the company.

Helpful Hints

Ask parents to save food boxes and labels from cans.

Laminate the labels for durability.

The labels and boxes can be taped to the table to make copying easier.

Children will read the labels and talk about their personal experiences using the product.

Some children may trace the letters and words on the labels.

Modifications

Plan the same activity using tracing paper, especially if children demonstrate an interest in tracing the letters and words.

Plan the same activity on a light table. Children will more easily see through the paper to trace the letters and words.

Comments & Questions to Extend Thinking

What label would you like to copy?

I like to eat granola bars. Can you find the granola bar box so that I can copy the words?

Detha is looking for peanut butter. Can you help her find that label?

Comments & Questions to Encourage Phonetic Awareness

"Tuna" and "taco" both begin with the same sound. Listen as I say each word.

"Cereal" and "soap" both begin with the "s" sound, but "cereal" begins with the letter "c."

Integrated Curriculum Activities

Plan a field trip to a local grocery store. Children can make a shopping list before they go and search for those items at the store.

Create a math game using novelty grocery items as the counters (see *Much More Than Counting*, activity 5.12).

Add the food labels to the writing center (activity 5.11).

7.15 Waiting List

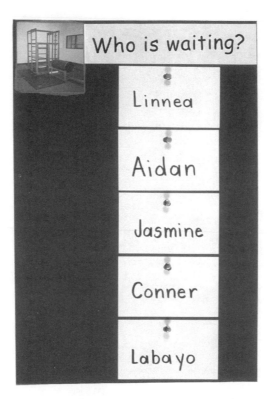

Who is waiting?

Linnea

Aidan

Jasmine

Conner

Labayo

Description

At school, children quickly learn that sometimes they have to wait for a turn. A waiting list helps children monitor how long they have to wait and reassures them that their turn won't be forgotten. This activity describes a waiting list for younger children who are just beginning to recognize their name but are not yet attempting to write it. The chart helps prepare children for a more traditional waiting list, which can be introduced later in the year (see Integrated Curriculum Activities, below). The photograph shows a waiting list for children who want to go to the gross-motor area of the school. Children hang their name cards on a chart designed in the form of a list.

Child's Level

This activity is appropriate for very young preschool children at the beginning of the year.

Materials

- poster board, 12 by 18 inches, in any color
- 3-by-5-inch index cards, each printed with the name of a child in the class

- photograph of the gross-motor room (or other area), to identify the waiting list for that area
- ¾-inch paper fasteners

What to Look For

Children will quickly recognize their names, just as they do in other areas of the classroom, but may not understand the concept of a waiting list. The teacher can model placing the child's name on the chart.

Children will place their names on the waiting-list chart but may not attend to the correct ordering of names.

Some children will place their names on the waiting-list chart in the appropriate order, from top to bottom.

A few children may change the order of the names to move themselves closer to the top of the list!

Modification

As the teacher observes emergent writing skills in individual children, the name cards can be removed (see chapter 1 for more information about writing). Children can write their names on slips of paper with prepunched holes and add them to the list in place of a name card.

Comments & Questions to Extend Thinking

Who is waiting for a turn next on the waiting list?

How many more children will have a turn before it is your turn?

You can use your name card to copy your name on the waiting list.

Comments & Questions to Encourage Phonetic Awareness

You want to write your name and Andy's name on the waiting list. What sound do you hear at the beginning of "Andy?" What letter do you think makes that sound?

Your name is after Megan on the waiting list. "Megan" starts with the letter "m," just like "Mom."

Integrated Curriculum Activities

Use children's names in many areas of the classroom (activities 7.1 through 7.4).

Sing songs with children's names (activity 3.1).

Later in the year the teacher can place clipboards, pencils, and paper at places in the room where only a limited number of children can be accommodated at one time. Children can sign their names to the clipboards and wait for their turns to use the area.

Helpful Hint

Punch several holes in the name cards to make them easier for children to hang on the chart.

7.16 Daily Message Board

Today we will walk to the grocery store.

Description

Children and parents enjoy reading a daily message from the teacher. Teachers often use the message board to describe the art activity for the day, announce a special visitor, or remind children about field trip permission forms. Parents may begin the transition by joining the child at the art activity, talking about the visitor, or turning in the permission form. This is a way for parents to help children transition into the classroom. Teachers can also plan a message for a specific child or children. For example, the teacher's message might suggest that several children look at the job chart, or it might encourage two children to investigate the pendulum in the science area. A wipe-off message board is pictured in the photograph above; however, a piece of paper can also be used.

Child's Level

This activity is appropriate for preschool, kindergarten, and first-grade children.

Materials

◆ small dry-erase board
◆ dry-erase markers

Helpful Hint

Odd-lot stores may be a source of inexpensive wipe-off boards.

What to Look For
Children and parents will eagerly read the message on the board.
Children will recognize letters and words on the message board.
Many children will respond to the statement or question written
on the message board.
Some children will contribute ideas for what to write on the
message board.

Modification
The message can be printed on the computer and taped to
the door.

Comments & Questions to Extend Thinking
Did you read the message on the door today?
This message has your name in it. I wonder what the
message says.
Will you read the message to Kate when she gets here?

Comments & Questions to Encourage Phonetic Awareness
Jacob thinks the message says we have a guest today. Ask him
which word he thinks is "guest." It starts with the same sound
as Garrett's name.
Let's try to figure out this word on the message board. The first
letter is "p, puh." Then I see "a" and "i" next to each other, "ay,"
and then "n" and "t." "Paint!"

Integrated Curriculum Activities
Make a message board like the one in activity 7.17. This may help
children focus on the function of print to communicate infor-
mation.
Write messages to children and put them in the literacy suitcases.
Children may become more interested in reading messages.

7.17 Class Message Board

Write a message.

Eden Brianna Sophie Tricia Christian

Bowen Samanatha Unique Andy Nitara

Casey La'Don Will James Alex

Brenda

Helpful Hints
Your school librarian may be willing to donate library pockets for the message board.

Library pockets are also available in office supply stores.

Use a mat knife to reopen the slit in the library pocket after lamination.

Description
A message board that is part of the classroom environment encourages children to communicate in writing to the teacher and to each other. This activity describes a message board made with a library pocket for each child glued to poster board. After lamination of the poster board, slits are cut to reopen the library pockets. Initially, not all children may want to write messages; however, they will be very excited to receive messages! Often, when children receive messages, they are motivated to write back to that person. This process encourages emergent writing and also provides samples for the teacher to use in assessing writing development.

Child's Level
This activity is appropriate for preschool, kindergarten, and first-grade children.

Materials

- poster board, large enough to accommodate a library pocket for each child and teacher in the class
- library pocket for each child in the class (each child's name is written on a pocket)
- laminating materials, to protect the message board

What to Look For

Children will recognize their names on the message board.

Children will ask the teacher to read the messages they receive.

Children will write messages to the teacher and other children using a variety of writing from scribbles to words and sentences.

Some children will dictate messages for others to the teacher.

Modification

Small envelopes can be used in place of the library pockets. Cut off the flap of the envelope before gluing it to the poster board. After laminating the chart, cut a slit in the lamination to reopen the envelope.

Comments & Questions to Extend Thinking

Do you have a message today? Look on the message board to find out.

I saw a note to you on the message board. Do you know who wrote to you?

You can write a note to me to remind me that you want to sit at my table for lunch tomorrow.

Comments & Questions to Encourage Phonetic Awareness

You want to ask Bowen to sit with you at lunch tomorrow. You can write your name, Bowen's name, and the word "lunch." Listen as I say the word "lunch." What sound do you hear at the beginning of the word?

Help me write a message to Dena. I want to tell her I will not be here Monday. The first letter of "Monday" makes a "muh" sound. What letter makes that sound?

Integrated Curriculum Activities

Plan other writing activities to encourage children to experiment with writing (see chapter 4).

Set up the dramatic play area as a post office, with supplies of paper, pencils, envelopes, pretend stamps, and individual mailboxes (activity 4.10).

CHAPTER 8

Literacy Suitcases

Casey reluctantly returned the literacy suitcase several days late. Her mother told the teacher that Casey had used every piece of paper in the suitcase. The mother also reported that Casey had not shown any interest in writing before she brought home the suitcase. Casey's teacher noticed an increased interest in the writing center after Casey returned the literacy suitcase.

▲ ▲ ▲

When Stephen returned the literacy suitcase, he insisted that his teacher open the envelope inside. He had written her a note that read, Brenda, Thank you for the suitcase. I love it. Stephen. *Stephen's father told the teacher that Stephen's older sister had helped him make the note. In the suitcase, the teacher found several writing samples, some written by Stephen and some obviously written by a much older child.*

▲ ▲ ▲

The literacy suitcase provides opportunities for children to explore writing materials, and it also enhances the home-school relationship. Children are very excited to take home the suitcase. Parents become more aware of the value of emergent writing explorations and observe their children engaged in writing activities. During the school year, parents may also observe changes in the child's interest and ability in writing.

Teachers' Questions

What is a literacy suitcase?

The literacy suitcase is a take-home version of the classroom writing center. It contains many of the same materials found in classroom writing centers and encourages children to explore these materials in their own homes. Some suitcases include a book or other materials that focus on emergent reading.

Why are literacy suitcases important?

Literacy suitcases encourage emergent writing in young children and build home-school relationships. Children progress through predictable stages in writing over a period of time. The literacy suitcase provides additional opportunities for the emergence of writing. The suitcase is enjoyable and nonthreatening. It educates parents about how children progress through the stages in writing. Chapter 1 contains detailed information about the stages in the emergence of writing in young children.

How have literacy suitcases evolved?

Literacy suitcases have evolved from supplies of general writing and art materials to suitcases focused primarily on writing activities. We designed our original literacy suitcases based on an article by Susan Rich (see "The Writing Suitcase" in *Young Children*, July 1985). She suggested that teachers send home paper, pencils, markers, tape, and a stapler to encourage children to write at home. While we noticed that children were excited to take the suitcase home, we also observed that many children used the materials for art collages and drawing activities rather than for writing explorations. For this reason, teachers began to experiment with variations of the suitcase. Some teachers removed all the art supplies; others included a small book in the suitcase. Some teachers included name cards for all the children in the group. We began to find more samples of children's writing in the suitcases returned to us. For example, many children began to produce marks that more closely resembled the linear form of writing rather than the circular form of drawing. Some children copied the name and word cards. Parents also provided us with valuable information about their children's emergent writing.

Why are literacy suitcases an important part of the curriculum?

Literacy suitcases encourage children to construct concepts related to the meaning of print and the mechanics of written communication. The suitcases also help teachers communicate valuable literacy-development information to parents. The literacy suitcase is a bridge between school and home. It educates parents about the value of exploring writing. In some cases, the literacy suitcase provides materials that may not be available at home.

How do literacy suitcases encourage children to construct the concepts related to writing?

Literacy suitcases provide writing supplies and accessories that encourage children to experiment with written communication. The name cards and word cards provide opportunities for children to copy meaningful print. These cards provide models of conventional print and motivate children to make successive approximations of the letters. Children enjoy copying their names and the names of others. They also enjoy copying words related to the book included in the suitcase. These explorations build a foundation for success in written communication.

What are the components of the literacy suitcase?

The basic components of the literacy suitcase include
- *a variety of sizes and types of paper*
- *a pencil*
- *name cards for the children in the class*
- *an alphabet sample*

Teachers should assess children's developmental levels to determine the contents of the suitcase. Additional supplies may be included to add variety and encourage more complex explorations of writing.

A parent letter briefly explains how children progress through the stages in writing. The letter cautions parents not to pressure children to write and not to correct their errors, but rather to assist children as they progress through the stages of emergent writing. A sample letter is included in appendix E.

A note to the child reinforces literacy concepts and tells the child when to return the suitcase. Some teachers use fancy note or shape paper for the message to children, as in the example below.

Sample Note to Child

Dear Claire,

Have fun with the writing suitcase. You can write messages to your friends. Please return the suitcase on Tuesday.

Love,
Brenda

What additional materials can teachers include in the literacy suitcase?

Teachers can add accessory materials to the suitcase, such as a board or paperback book, blank books, word cards, and fill-in-the-blank papers. These are the same accessories teachers often add to the basic writing center in the classroom. Chapter 5 describes how to make these materials. Teachers may occasionally include markers, crayons, envelopes, and tape. Children often use markers and crayons in the same way as they use pencils to experiment with writing. Some children may make their own small books using the paper and tape.

What should teachers avoid including in the literacy suitcase?

Teachers should avoid including art supplies, such as glue and scissors, in the suitcase. The inclusion of these art materials may encourage some children to focus more attention on art activities rather than on writing explorations. Children sometimes use art supplies for cutting and gluing activities. The suitcase might come back with name cards cut in half or glued together!

Where can teachers find the supplies for literacy suitcases?

Teachers can find small plastic school boxes in the school-supplies section of many discount stores. Paper and pencils, as well as supplies for making name and word cards, are available through school-supply catalogs. Other suggestions for the literacy suitcase include a small lunch box, an empty craft box, a backpack, or even an old briefcase. Chapter 5 gives a detailed description of the types of paper and pencils to provide for writing activities. The activities in this chapter show many examples of different combinations of supplies.

How do teachers plan what to include in the suitcase?

Teachers should evaluate the age range and experience of the group as well as the developmental levels of individual children. If a child is not yet experimenting with writing in the classroom, the teacher may send home a basic literacy suitcase to stimulate interest in writing (activity 8.1). This basic suitcase is often the first type sent home with children. If a child demonstrates high interest in copying letters and words at the writing center, the teacher may include a book and word cards related to the book. The suitcase may also contain fill-in-the-blank papers. Teachers of kindergarten children may select more complex accessories, such as story starters or small journals for record keeping. Suggestions for different levels of literacy suitcases are found in the activities in this chapter.

Teachers often select predictable books to include in the literacy suitcase. Books with a predictable story structure provide opportunities for teachers to select high-interest words for the word cards included in the suitcase. For example, the book *Dear Zoo,* by Rod Campbell (Washington, DC: Four Winds, 1982) is appropriate, contains a predictable sentence, and focuses on zoo animals. The teacher can make word cards to coordinate with the specific animals in the book. Children are typically very interested in the story and enjoy reading the names of the animals and attempting to copy those high-interest words.

How do age levels affect what is included in literacy suitcases?

Younger, less-experienced children benefit from a smaller selection of writing materials, while older, more-experienced children are ready for more elaborate writing accessories. A younger child may not make appropriate use of a literacy suitcase that contains a large quantity of supplies or developmentally inappropriate materials. Likewise, a more-experienced child may become bored if the literacy suitcase is too basic for the child's developmental level and interests.

How can teachers adapt the literacy suitcase for children with disabilities?

Teachers can modify the type of materials, the format of the materials, and the quantities of materials included in the suitcase to meet the needs of children with disabilities. Teachers may include a photograph of each child on the name cards for a child with a cognitive delay. Some teachers include this for all children, since it is very appealing. Teachers may also reduce the quantities of supplies for children with cognitive or physical delays to ensure a more successful writing experience. Picture cards for sign-language symbols can be included for children who are communicating using signs. For children with low muscle tone, teachers might include a pencil that is only about three and a half inches long. This helps children hold the pencil in a more mature grasp rather than an overhand or fisted grip. Teachers may modify the word cards for children with a visual disability by enlarging the print or highlighting letters in puffy paints. In some cases, the teacher might use a Braille machine to create word cards. A tape recording of the book might be included for non-English-speaking children.

How often do children take literacy suitcases home?

Each child takes the suitcase home several times each year. The suitcases go home on a rotating basis. Our classrooms each have sixteen children. Some teachers send home one suitcase per week, while others send home more each week. Children get a turn once or twice every few months. Since children are typically very excited to take home the literacy suitcase, some teachers post a schedule so that children know when their turn is coming. Teachers often send the suitcase home on Thursdays and ask children to return it on Mondays or Tuesdays. This allows teachers several days to replenish the supplies for the next child.

How can teachers assess children's writing development using the literacy suitcase?

Teachers can collect and preserve artifacts from the literacy suitcase. These writing samples often amplify the information already recorded by the teacher based on observations in the classroom. Some children may not feel comfortable attempting to produce letters at school but may readily do so at home. Children who do not select the writing materials in the classroom may demonstrate advanced skills based on samples from their explorations at home. Some teachers post the writing samples in the classroom and later include them in the child's portfolio, school file, or end-of-the-year scrapbook.

Literacy-Suitcase Activities

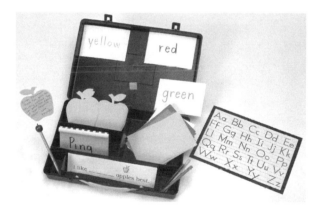

8.1 The Basic Literacy Suitcase

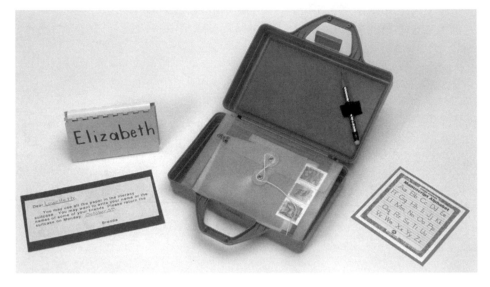

Description

This basic literacy suitcase contains a generous supply of materials for writing experiences. Teachers might choose this type of literacy suitcase to introduce at the beginning of the year, for children who enter after the start of school, or for specific children with cognitive delays.

Child's Level

The materials in this literacy suitcase are appropriate for preschool and kindergarten children at the beginning of the year.

Materials

- ◆ various colors of duplicating paper (quarter-sheets)
- ◆ recycled envelopes and advertisement stamps from various organizations, book clubs, and record clubs
- ◆ fancy pencil
- ◆ name cards for all the children and teachers in the class (print the names on index cards, laminate, and bind or hold together with a notebook ring)
- ◆ alphabet sample
- ◆ note to parents about the suitcase
- ◆ note to the child

Helpful Hint

Review the content of the stamps for objectionable print or pictures.

What to Look For

Children will experiment with the writing materials.
Some children will draw and write.
Some children will use *all* the supplies in the suitcase.
Some children will write their name using their current stage of
    development in writing.
A few children may not use any of the supplies.

Modifications

A picture of each child can be glued to each name card
    before lamination.
Reduce or increase the quantities of supplies to fit the
    developmental level of the individual child.
Include a small board or paperback book.

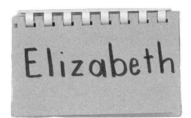

Integrated Curriculum Activities

Include a copy of the book used in the suitcase in the classroom.
Place writing caddies around the classroom (activity 4.18).

8.2 Apple Literacy Suitcase

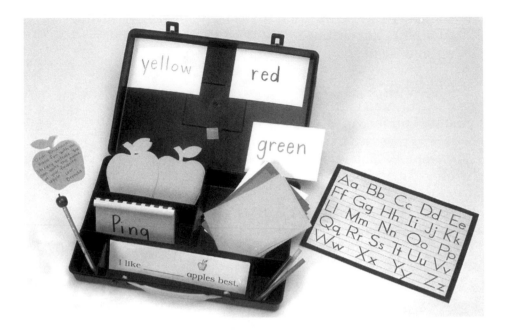

Description

During autumn, many early childhood programs plan activities such as apple tasting, apple printing, making applesauce, and perhaps a field trip to pick apples. The grocery store typically has a large selection of apples, including Granny Smith and red and golden delicious. Children are familiar with apples as a snack and lunch food. This suitcase may build on classroom experiences with apples; however, it is equally appealing to children without those experiences. It is more complex than a basic literacy suitcase but does not contain a book or a story starter.

Child's Level

This literacy suitcase is most appropriate for preschool and kindergarten children.

Materials

- yellow, green, red, and white photocopy paper (quarter-sheets)
- apple pencil, or red pencil decorated with several apple stickers
- red, yellow, and green crayons or colored pencils
- name cards for all the children and teachers in the class (see activity 8.1)
- word cards for red, yellow, and green, written in the appropriate color of marker

Helpful Hint

Restaurants often supply crayons at the table for children. Ask parents to save these for you.

- fill-in-the-blank papers (4 to 6) that read *I like ___ apples best.*
- apple-shaped paper
- alphabet sample
- note to the child

What to Look For

Children will experiment with the writing
   materials.
Some children will copy the color words.
Some children will copy the color words onto
   the fill-in papers.
Some children may copy their names and the
   names of other children.

Modification

Add three or four blank books, made with an
   apple sticker or rubber-stamp impression on
   the original and duplicated on colored paper.

Integrated Curriculum Activities

Taste apples and graph the children's favorites (see *More Than
   Counting,* activity 6.5).
Provide apple-shaped sponges and cookie cutters for a painting
   activity (see *More Than Painting,* activity 5.17).
Estimate how many seeds are in an apple. Then open one and
   count them (see *Much More Than Counting,* activity 3.6).
Peel apples for a cooking experience using a hand-turned apple
   peeler (see *More Than Magnets,* activity 7.2).

8.3 Autumn Literacy Suitcase

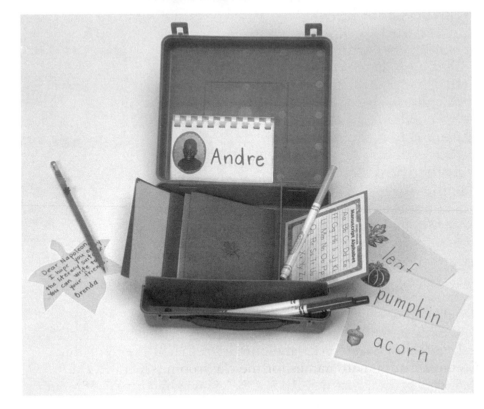

Description
This suitcase contains autumn words and is appropriate to plan during the first several months of school. Since some teachers send home two literacy suitcases each week, this one and the apple suitcase would be appropriate choices to plan at the same time.

Child's Level
This literacy suitcase is most appropriate for preschool and kindergarten children.

Materials
- white, yellow, green, red, and orange photocopy paper (quarter-sheets)
- yellow pencil, decorated with several leaf stickers
- red, yellow, orange, brown, and green thin markers
- name cards for all the children and teachers in the class (see activity 8.1)

- alphabet sample
- word cards for *leaf, squirrel, acorn,* and *pumpkin*
- illustrations of a leaf, a squirrel, an acorn, and a pumpkin, for the word cards
- 3 or 4 blank books, made with autumn stickers or rubber-stamp impressions on the original and duplicated on red, yellow, green, and orange paper
- note to the child

What to Look For

Children will experiment with the writing materials.

Some children will copy the autumn words.

Some children may copy their name and the names of other children.

Some children may copy some of the alphabet sample into the blank books.

Modification

Add an autumn book to the suitcase, such as *Fresh Fall Leaves,* by Betsy Franco (New York: Scholastic, 1994).

Integrated Curriculum Activities

Include autumn books in the classroom, such as *Nuts to You,* by Lois Ehlert (New York: Harcourt, 1993).

Create autumn math games for the classroom (see *More Than Counting,* activities 2.5, 3.15, 4.5, 4.6, 4.13, 5.7, and 5.18).

8.4 The Mitten Literacy Suitcase

Description
This more complex literacy suitcase coordinates with the Ukrainian folktale "The Mitten" and the interactive poem chart based on the book (activity 3.4). The larger quantity of word cards and fill-in-the blank papers may be overwhelming for younger or less-experienced children. A note from the teacher encourages children to experiment with writing the names of additional animals that crawl into the mitten. Children can use invented spelling or look for models for conventional spellings of the names.

Helpful Hints

The illustrations of the animals can be found at Jan Brett's Web site.

Use the computer to produce the fill-in sheet original, since it requires a long sentence.

Child's Level
This suitcase is appropriate for older preschool, kindergarten, and first-grade children. The modifications would make it appropriate for younger children as well.

Materials
- white and blue photocopy paper (quarter-sheets)
- recycled envelopes and advertisement stamps from various organizations and book or record clubs
- fancy pencil
- name cards for all the children and teachers in the class (see activity 8.1)
- alphabet sample

- word cards, for the animals in a book version of "The Mitten"
- illustrations of the animals, for the word cards
- 3 or 4 blank books, made with a mitten cutout on the original and duplicated on paper
- fill-in-the-blank papers that read *In crawled* _____ , *which made the mitten grow.*
- note to the child

What to Look For

Some children will copy all the animal names from the word cards.

Some children may copy their names, the names of other children, or the names of family members onto the fill-in papers. They often think this is a great joke.

Children will write in a variety of ways, such as personal cursive or letterlike forms, depending on their stage of development.

Some children will write the animal names in the spaces on the fill-in papers.

Some children will think of different animal names to write on the fill-in papers.

Modification

Add a note from the teacher that encourages children to think of additional animals that might crawl into the mitten.

Integrated Curriculum Activities

Include a book version of the story, such as *The Mitten,* by Jan Brett (New York: Putnam, 1989), in the classroom.

Create a gross-motor math game based on *The Mitten* (see *Much More Than Counting,* activity 1.15).

8.5 Post-Office Literacy Suitcase

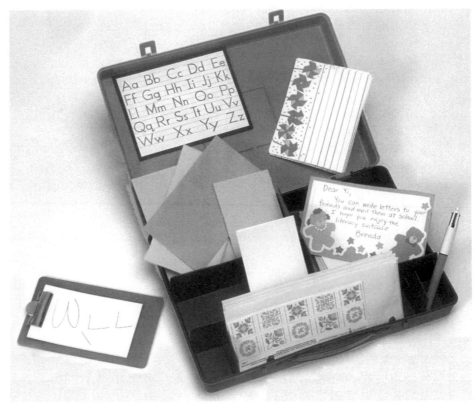

Description

Many early childhood programs set up a post office in the dramatic play area to encourage children to experiment with writing, as well as act out the role of the mail carrier (see activity 4.10). This post-office literacy suitcase coordinates well with a class post office. Although the literacy suitcase is appropriate for any time of the year, teachers might want to plan it around Valentine's Day.

Child's Level

This literacy suitcase is most appropriate for older preschool, kindergarten, and first-grade children.

Materials

- various colors of photocopy paper, index cards, lined paper, and inexpensive writing pads
- different sizes and colors of envelopes
- advertisement stamps from various organizations and book or record clubs

Helpful Hint

Card stores often have extra envelopes without cards. Ask someone to save these for you.

- ball point pen, with several colors of ink in one pen
- first and last names and addresses of all the teachers and children in the class, perhaps in an inexpensive address book or teacher-made address book
- alphabet sample
- note to the child

What to Look For
Children will experiment with the writing materials.
Some children will copy the first names of other children.
Some children may copy the first and last names of other children.
Some children may copy names and addresses on the envelopes.
Some children will write in a letter format, with *Dear* _____ , at the top of the paper or index card.

Modification
Include some papers preprinted with *Dear* _____ , at the top to encourage children to write in the form of a letter.

Integrated Curriculum Activities
Create a class mail book (activity 2.5).
Let children send messages home. They can walk to a mailbox in small groups and mail them.
Send this suitcase home around Valentine's Day and include supplies for making holiday cards. The word cards duplicate the phrases found on candy hearts, such as *Be Mine* and *Best Friends*.

8.6 Sleepy-Animals Literacy Suitcase

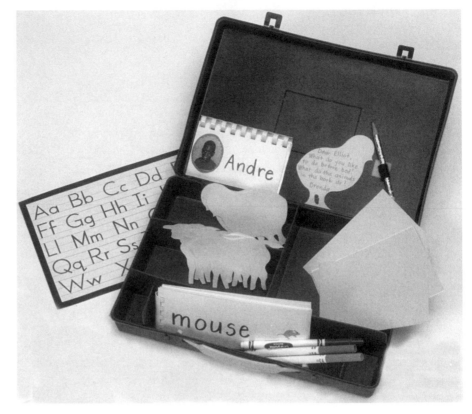

Description
This literacy suitcase coordinates with the poetic book *Time for Bed,* by Mem Fox (New York: Harcourt, 1997). The poems describe the bedtime routine of various animal families.

Child's Level
This literacy suitcase is most appropriate for preschool and kindergarten children.

Materials
- pastel photocopy paper (quarter-sheets)
- iridescent or laser-cut pencil
- several thin markers
- name card for all the children and teachers in the class (see activity 8.1)
- alphabet sample
- word cards, for the animals in the book
- illustrations of the animals in the book, for the word cards
- paper cutouts of some of the animals in the book

Helpful Hint

Ellison cutouts match many of the animals in the book.

- ◆ note to the child
- ◆ copy of the book *Time for Bed*

What to Look For
Children will experiment with the writing materials.
Some children will draw and write.
Some children will copy the animal words into the
blank books.
Some children may copy their name and the names of
other children.

Modifications
Add fill-in-the blank papers with the words *It's time for
bed, little _____.*
Include four or five blank books in the suitcase.

Integrated Curriculum Activities
Place writing caddies around the classroom (activity 4.18).
Include animal families in the block area for sorting and classify-
ing (see *Much More Than Counting*, activity 1.7).
Clap animal words for a rhythm activity (see *More Than Singing*,
chapter 3).
Create an animal path game for a math activity (see *Much More
Than Counting*, activity 7.4b).

8.7 "I Love You" Literacy Suitcase

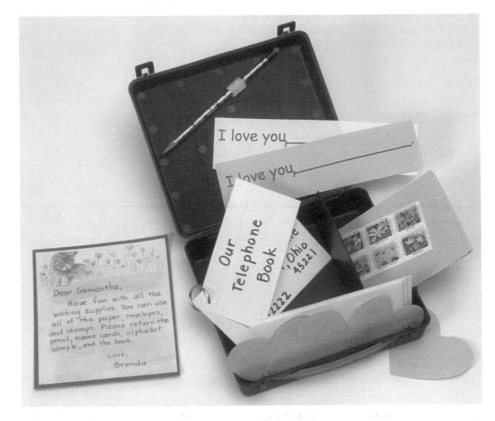

Description
This literacy suitcase coordinates with the book *I Love You, Sun, I Love You, Moon,* by Karen Pandell (New York: Scholastic, 1994). It includes interesting materials that can be sent home around Valentine's Day for younger children. It does not include word cards, blank books, or other extra writing materials that may be overwhelming to younger children.

Child's Level
This literacy suitcase is most appropriate for young preschool children.

Materials
- pink, lavender, and white photocopy paper (quarter-sheets)
- recycled envelopes and advertisement stamps from various organizations and book or record clubs
- iridescent or laser-cut pencil
- name card for all the children and teachers in the class (see activity 8.1)

Helpful Hint

Wrap a piece of self-adhesive Velcro around the pencil. Attach another piece inside the suitcase to keep the pencil with the case.

- alphabet sample
- heart-shaped paper
- fill-in-the-blank papers that read *I love you, _____.*
- copy of the book *I Love You, Sun, I Love You, Moon*
- note to the child

What to Look For

Children will experiment with the writing
   materials.
Some children will use all the supplies in the
   suitcase.
Some children will write their names using their
   current stage of development in writing.
Some children will copy their names and the
   names of other children onto the fill-in papers.
A few children may not use any of the supplies.
Many children will bring back messages in the
   envelopes for their friends.

Modification

Include several rolls of inexpensive colored tape
   and a stapler along with a note to the child. The note can suggest that the child use the heart paper, tape, and stapler to make
   cards for friends.

Integrated Curriculum Activities

Include *I Love You, Sun, I Love You, Moon* in the reading area of
   the classroom.
Design a math game with ice cube trays and heart-shaped refreez-
   able ice shapes (see *More Than Counting,* activity 2.3).

8.8 Cloud Literacy Suitcase

Description

The cloud literacy suitcase provides opportunities for children to copy word cards based on the book *It Looked Like Spilt Milk,* by Charles G. Shaw (New York: Harper, 1947). It also encourages them to use invented spelling to write the names of cloud formations they observe or imagine.

Child's Level

This literacy suitcase is appropriate for preschool, kindergarten, and first-grade children.

Materials

◆ white and blue duplicating paper (quarter-sheets)
◆ paper cut into random cloud shapes with wavy scissors
◆ light blue pencil
◆ name card for all the children and teachers in the class (see activity 8.1)
◆ alphabet sample
◆ word cards, for the shapes of the cloud formations in the book
◆ illustrations of the shapes of the cloud formations, for the word cards
◆ 3 or 4 blank books, made with a cloud cutout on the original and duplicated on blue and white paper
◆ fill-in-the-blank papers that read "It looked like _____."
◆ note to the child

Helpful Hint

Include an outline of a cloud on the original fill-in-the-blank paper.

What to Look For

Some children will write all the cloud formation names into the blank books.

Some children may copy their names, the names of other children, or family members onto the fill-in papers.

Children will write in a variety of ways, such as personal cursive or letterlike forms, depending on their stage of development.

Some children will write the cloud formation names on the fill-in papers.

Some children will use invented spelling to write on the fill-in papers.

Modification

Include a small picture dictionary in the suitcase. Children can copy words they choose to describe clouds.

an Ice Cream Cone

It looked like_____.

Dear Shoshana
Have fun with the Cloud Literacy suitcase
What do you see when you look at the clouds?
Love,
Brenda

Integrated Curriculum Activities

Sing a cloud song (see *More Than Singing*, activity 2.8).

Plan a collage activity using white fiberfill on blue paper (see *More Than Painting*, activity 7.15).

8.9 Farm Literacy Suitcase

Description
Young children frequently know the names of many farm animals. Very young children enjoy pointing to pictures of farm animals and imitating the sounds they make. Older children might like to copy the animal word cards or generate lists of other farm animals.

Child's Level
This literacy suitcase is most appropriate for preschool and kindergarten children.

Materials
- various colors of photocopy paper (quarter-sheets)
- reused envelopes and advertisement stamps from various organizations and book or record clubs
- red or other color pencil
- several thin markers
- name card for all the children and teachers in the class (see activity 8.1)

Helpful Hint
Computer-generated clip art is a good resource for illustrations of farm animals.

- alphabet sample
- word cards, for farm animals
- stickers or illustrations of farm animals, for the word cards
- 3 or 4 blank books, made with a farm animal sticker on the original and duplicated on various colors of paper
- note to the child

What to Look For

Children will experiment with the writing materials.
Some children will draw and write.
Some children will copy the animal words into the blank books.
Some children may copy their name and the names of other children.

Modification

This suitcase coordinates well with the books *This Is the Farmer*, by Nancy Tafuri (New York: Greenwillow, 1994), and *Wake Up, Wake Up,* by Brian and Rebecca Wildsmith (San Diego: Harcourt, 1993). Teachers may want to include one of them in the suitcase.

Integrated Curriculum Activities

Include other farm books in the classroom, such as *The Very Busy Spider,* by Eric Carle (New York: Philomel, 1984), and *The Big Fat Worm,* by Nancy Van Laan (New York: Knopf, 1987).
Include farm animals in the block area.
Plan a field trip to a local petting zoo that has small farm animals on display.
Create an "Old MacDonald" big book (activity 2.10).

Appendix A

Selected Predictable Books

Aliki. *Hush, Little Baby*. New York: Simon & Schuster, 1968.

Balian, Lorna. *Humbug Witch*. Nashville: Abingdon Press, 1965.

Benjamin, Cynthia. *Footprints in the Snow*. New York: Scholastic, 1994.

Barton, Byron. *Bones, Bones, Dinosaur Bones*. New York: Thomas Y. Crowell, 1990.

Barton, Byron, *Dinosaurs, Dinosaurs*. New York: Thomas Y. Crowell, 1989.

Barton, Byron, *I Want to Be an Astronaut*. New York: Thomas Y. Crowell, 1988.

Brown, Margaret Wise, *Goodnight Moon*. New York: Harper & Row, 1947.

Campbell, Rod, *Dear Zoo*. New York: Simon & Schuster, 1982.

Carle, Eric, *The Very Busy Spider*. New York: Philomel, 1984.

Carle, Eric, *The Very Hungry Caterpillar*. New York: Philomel, 1969.

Crews, Donald, *Flying*. New York: Greenwillow, 1986.

Crews, Donald, *Freight Train*. New York: Mulberry, 1978.

Dalton, Anne, *This Is the Way*. New York: Scholastic, 1992.

Emberley, Barbara, *Drummer Hoff*. New York: Prentice-Hall, 1967.

Fleming, Denise, *Barnyard Banter*. New York: Henry Holt, 1994.

Fleming, Denise, *Mama Cat Has Three Kittens*. New York: Henry Holt, 1998.

Fox, Mem, *Hattie and the Fox*. New York: Bradbury Press, 1987.

Fox, Mem, *Time for Bed*. San Diego: Harcourt Brace, 1993.

Fox, Mem, *Tough Boris*. San Diego: Harcourt Brace, 1994.

Gilman, Phoebe, *Something from Nothing*. New York: Scholastic, 1992.

Gomi, Taro, *My Friends*. San Francisco: Chronicle Books, 1990.

Ho, Minfong, *Hush!* New York: Orchard Books, 1996.

Hutchins, Pat, *The Doorbell Rang*. New York: Greenwillow, 1986.

Hutchins, Pat, *Good-Night Owl*. New York: Simon & Schuster, 1972.

Hutchins, Pat, *My Best Friend*. New York: Greenwillow, 1993.

Hutchins, Pat, *Rosie's Walk*. New York: Macmillan, 1968.

Hutchins, Pat, *Titch*. New York: Macmillan, 1971.

Hutchins, Pat, *The Wind Blew*. New York: Macmillan, 1974.

Hutchins, Pat, *You'll Soon Grow into Them, Titch*. New York: Greenwillow, 1983.

Jonas, Ann, *Color Dance*. New York: Greenwillow, 1989.

Kalan, Robert, *Blue Sea*. New York: Greenwillow, 1979.

Kalan, Robert, *Jump, Frog, Jump!* New York: Greenwillow, 1981.

Krauss, Ruth, *The Carrot Seed*. New York: Harper & Row, 1945.

Langstaff, John, *Oh, A-Hunting We Will Go*. New York: Macmillan, 1974.

Leventhal, Debra, *What Is Your Language?* New York: Dutton, 1994.

Mack, Stan, *10 Bears in My Bed*. New York: Pantheon, 1974.

Martin, Bill, *Brown Bear, Brown Bear, What Do You See?* New York: Henry Holt, 1983.

Martin, Bill, *Chicka Chicka Boom Boom*. New York: Simon & Schuster, 1989.

Morgan, Pierr, *The Turnip*. New York: Philomel, 1990.

Peek, Merle, *Mary Wore Her Red Dress*. New York: Clarion, 1985.

Porter-Gaylord, Laurel, *I Love My Daddy Because . . .* New York: Dutton, 1991.

Porter-Gaylord, Laurel, *I Love My Mommy Because . . .* New York: Dutton, 1991.

Raffi, *Shake My Sillies Out*. New York: Crown, 1987.

Raffi, *Tingalayo*. New York: Crown, 1989.

Raffi, *Wheels on the Bus*. New York: Crown, 1988.

Rosen, Michael, *We're Going on a Bear Hunt*. New York: Simon & Schuster, 1989.

Shaw, Charles G., *It Looked Like Spilt Milk*. New York: Harper & Row, 1947.

Titherington, Jeanne, *Pumpkin, Pumpkin*. New York: Greenwillow, 1986.

Trapani, Iza, *The Itsy Bitsy Spider*. New York: Scholastic, 1993.

Waddell, Martin, *Owl Babies*. Cambridge, MA: Candlewick Press, 1992.

Ward, Leila, *I Am Eyes, Ni Macho*. New York: Greenwillow, 1978.

Wildsmith, Brian and Rebecca, *Wake Up, Wake Up!* San Diego: Harcourt Brace, 1993.

Williams, Sue, *I Went Walking*. San Diego: Harcourt Brace, 1989.

Williams, Vera B., *"More More More," Said the Baby*. New York: Greenwillow, 1990.

Westcott, Nadine Bernard, *The Lady with the Alligator Purse*. Boston: Little Brown, 1988.

Wood, Audrey, *I'm As Quick As a Cricket*. Singapore: Child's Play, 1982.

Wood, Audrey, *King Bidgood's in the Bathtub*. San Diego: Harcourt Brace, 1985.

Wood, Audrey, *The Napping House*. San Diego: Harcourt Brace, 1984.

Wood, Audrey, *Silly Sally*. San Diego: Harcourt Brace, 1992.

Ziefert, Harriet, *Where's the Halloween Treat?* New York: Puffin, 1985.

Appendix B

Alphabet Model

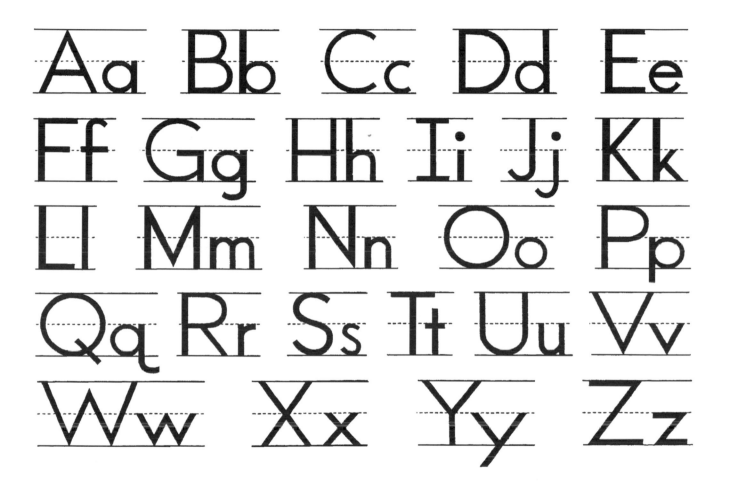

Appendix C: Reading Assessment

Terms and Definitions for Reading Assessment

Term	Definition
letter/word recognition	
own name	recognizes own name (from a group of 1–3, 4–8, or more than 8 names) initially by first letter only
other names	recognizes names of others (from a group of 1–3, 4–8, or more than 8 names) initially by first letter only
letters	recognizes letters in a variety of situations (name cards, ABC sample, books, charts, signs, and labels)
words	recognizes familiar words in print; initially may need picture cue (*open, closed, exit, marker, tape,* and so on)
reading strategies	
sound–symbol	makes connection between letter or cluster of letters and a specific sound (uses strategy to read new words)
voice–print	points to each written word while saying the word
predicts from text	guesses what word or phrase comes next in a book or on a chart
reading outcomes	
pretends to read	turns pages, uses inflection, points to words, and so on (may pretend to read to another child or stuffed animal)
retells stories	retells familiar story in his own words, with some book words or phrases (may use story props)
remembers phrases	chimes in with repetitive phrase from book, poem, or song chart
reads words	reads familiar or unfamiliar words without picture cues (no books, charts, signs, labels, or other environmental print)
reads new books	reads an unfamiliar book

Reading Assessment Form

Child:

date	material	letter/word recognition		reading strategies			reading outcomes					comments
		own name	other names	letters	words	sound–symbol	voice–print	predicts from context	pretends to read	retells stories	remem-bers phrases	reads words	reads new books	

©2001 More Than Letters; Redleaf Press ◆ 450 North Syndicate, Suite 5, St. Paul, MN 55104 ◆ 800-423-8309

Sample Reading Assessment Form

Child: *Wesley*

date	material	letter/word recognition				reading strategies			reading outcomes					comments
		own name	other names	letters	words	sound–symbol	voice–print	predicts from context	pretends to read	retells stories	remem-bers phrases	reads words	reads new books	
9/15	name cards	X												initially selects Will
9/24	attendance chart			X										A C F T W Z
10/1	name cards	X												"There's my W."
10/12	book "I Went Walking"								X					
10/14	book "I Went Walking"							X	X					"What did you see?"
10/27	attendance chart		X	X										eight names plus B H P
11/8	book "Big Fat Worm"										X			"Oh, no you're not," with expression
11/10	ABC sample		X	X										E L O S – writing center
11/13	interactive chart						X							attempts, but not accurate

©2001 *More Than Letters*; Redleaf Press ◆ 450 North Syndicate, Suite 5, St. Paul, MN 55104 ◆ 800-423-8309

Appendix D: Writing Assessment

Terms and Definitions for Writing Assessment

Term	Definition
writing stages	
scribbling	creates controlled scribbles to represent writing
linear repetitive drawing	makes horizontal, wavy lines to represent writing
letterlike forms	creates approximations of letters or forms that almost look like letters
letters	reproduces letters; single letter often represents entire word
invented spelling	writes a letter or letters to represent the sounds in a word
standard spelling	knows some standard spellings of words
hand grasp	
hand used	hand(s) that the child uses in the activity
fist grip	writing grasp in which child wraps four fingers around writing implement
overhand grip	writing grasp in which child wraps four fingers around writing implement, with back of hand facing child
three-finger grip	writing grasp in which child places two fingers on one side of the writing implement and the thumb opposite
tripod grip	standard writing grasp characterized by one finger on top of the writing implement, one finger below the writing implement, and the thumb opposite
writing outcomes	
copies print	refers to a child who copies print while looking at a model
prints without model	refers to a child who can write letters without first looking at a model
writes to communicate	refers to a child who writes, at whatever stage, with a clear desire to communicate meaning

Writing Assessment Form

Child: _____

date	material	writing stages						hand grasp					writing outcomes			comments
		scrib-bling	linear repeti-tive	letter-like	letters	invented spelling	standard spelling	hand used L/R	fist	over-hand	three-finger	tripod	copies print	prints without model	writes to commun-icate	

Sample Writing Assessment Form

Child: *Mary*

date	material	writing stages						hand grasp						writing outcomes			comments
		scrib-bling	linear repeti-tive	letter-like	letters	invented spelling	standard spelling	hand used L/R	fist	over-hand	three-finger	tripod	copies print	prints without model	writes to commun-icate	
10/1	class book		X					R			X					
10/4	lunch note		X	X				R			X				X	filled in space with wavy lines; said she wrote her name
10/10	writing caddy			X				R			X					said she wanted to sit by Amy
11/8	writing center			X	X			R				X				put letterlike forms in an apple blank book
11/15	lunch note							R				X			X	wrote "Ma" for her name

©2001 *More Than Letters*; Redleaf Press ◆ 450 North Syndicate, Suite 5, St. Paul, MN 55104 ◆ 800-423-8309

Appendix E

Literacy Suitcase

Sample Teacher Letter to Parent

Dear _____,

Today your child is bringing home a literacy suitcase. It contains a supply of paper, name cards for the children and teachers in the class, a small book, an alphabet sample, and a pencil. These are similar to the classroom materials your child uses to experiment with writing.

Young children practice writing long before they learn to produce letters and words. This is similar to the way children practice talking before they learn to speak in sentences. Remember all the funny mistakes your child made while learning to talk? Children also make mistakes while learning to write. Young children go through a series of stages in writing, from scribble to recognizable letters and words. Those initials scribbles are similar to the babbling of babies. Later, young children make some marks that look a little more like letters. This can be compared to the language of young children who can say a few words, even though they make mistakes. Remember how you laughed when your toddler said "wello" instead of "yellow" or used one word to mean five different things? Young children learn to copy letters and words, and before long they remember how to write the letters without a model. This is similar to when toddlers repeat or copy the language they hear. Eventually, young children produce unique sentences they have never heard before.

The mistakes children make as they learn to write and talk are a natural part of development. Parents are usually very excited when children begin to talk, even when they can't understand a single word! I hope you will be just as excited about your child's first attempts at writing, even when you can't read a single word!

Your child may keep the literacy suitcase until _____. Please bring it back then so that I can replace the supplies for the next child's turn. I do not expect the paper to be returned, but I appreciate your help in returning the name cards, small book, alphabet sample, and pencil. If you have any supplies that you would like to add to the suitcase, such as index cards or fancy paper, please feel free to do so. Enjoy writing with your child.

Also in the More Than . . . Series

More Than Counting – Math is so easy that children can do it, if we let them! Over 100 ideas for unusual and new manipulatives, collections, grid games, path games, graphing, and gross-motor play that combine to make a complete math experience. A teacher-friendly resource.

More Than Magnets – More than 100 activities engage children in interactive science in many areas of the classroom. Prepares teachers and caregivers to ask and answer questions. Includes life science, physics, and chemistry activities.

More Than Painting – Make art a thought-provoking, fun part of your everyday curriculum. *More Than Painting* provides an impressive variety of art activities (over 100) for the classroom. Activities include drawing, collage, painting and printing, sewing and stringing, three-dimensional art, and outdoor art.

More Than Singing – Over 100 activities and ideas for songs, instrument making, music centers, and extensions into language, science, and math. Clear directions and musical notations guide you. The cassette contains songs accompanied by guitar or Autoharp. Includes original songs and songs for movement and transitions.

Much More Than Counting – Contains more than 100 activities that will make math more fun for children. This book addresses those questions most asked by teachers, providers, and parents, as well as questions about toddlers, children with disabilities, estimation, and patterning—topics that often are forgotten in an early math curriculum. Each of the activities is accompanied by a photograph and a detailed explanation of how to set up the activity or construct materials.

Call Redleaf Press toll-free
to order or to request a catalog

800-423-8309
www.redleafpress.org